THERE IS
NO END

The first literary anthology by
Scribe: The Riverbend Writers Group

Edited by Mike Robertson

ISBN-13: 978-1461151005

ISBN-10: 1461151007

First printing • 1000 copies • July 2011

Riverbend Church
4214 N. Capital of Texas Hwy.
Austin, TX 78746

www.riverbend.com
Visit the Scribe blog at www.riverbendscribe.blogspot.com

*This book is dedicated to the
wonderful members of SCRIBE.
You are the reasons this book exists.
May you follow every dream with the
enthusiasm you brought to this one.*

INTRODUCTION

Riverbend Church has a commitment to the arts that is different from most churches. We believe that you are never more like your Creator than when you create. Over the years, this philosophy has brought many of the best musicians anywhere to our stage to share their talents with an appreciative audience. We opened our own art gallery to give exposure to visual artists whose work needed to be seen. But we are still growing into this commitment we've made.

Just over a year ago, a woman named Kathy Sargent met with our senior pastor, Dave Haney, and me. She wondered why we had not embraced writers in the same way we welcomed musicians and painters. There was no acceptable answer; we just hadn't gotten around to it or found the way to do it. Kathy and I met a couple more times to talk about what a writers group at Riverbend would look like. The result was the group we call Scribe.

Scribe is a group for anyone who has ever wished to be a writer. We meet twice a month, on the second and fourth Saturdays, at 11:00am in Quad 4. Sometimes we have guest authors come and speak to us; other times we take turns reading something we've written and getting feedback and critiques from our fellow writers.

I think most of the Scribe members would say they have been inspired by the group. For me, I was inspired to dust off a novel I'd finished years ago. I had grown tired of the arduous process of seeking publication. But things had changed in the intervening years. In the same way that computers have allowed us all to record music and make movies, the tools for writing and publishing a book are now within reach for almost everyone. I self-published my novel through Amazon.com and found the process virtually painless.

That gave me an idea. There's nothing more inspiring for a writer than seeing your name on a book, reading your work aloud at a release party, signing a copy of the book you wrote. I wanted to share that feeling with the Scribe tribe. I announced that we would publish an anthology of work by our own writers. I set a limit of 2500 words, picked a deadline date, and waited.

I was absolutely delighted by what happened. Nearly 90 pieces were submitted. I've picked my favorites and they're just a couple of pages from here. The variety was wonderful. There were the expected inspirational essays (hey, we're a church, after all), but there were poems, short stories, memoirs, even some ventures into travel, mystery, and romance. This is Forrest Gump's box of chocolates; you never know what you're gonna get. If one piece doesn't grab you, just flip over a page or two and you'll find something completely different. In assembling this book, I got to see a couple dozen people get excited about their own God-given talents…some for the first time.

That's a winning situation, but this one gets even better. I decided that all proceeds from the sale of this book would go to Riverbend's current building program. This is what I'd call a win/win/win situation: our authors get their work published and read, Riverbend gets to continue to improve our facilities, and you get to read a lot of great work by some people you may know!

While I have made some brief editorial remarks at the beginning of each piece in this book, you should also check out the brief biographies each writer submitted, which are printed in the last few pages. You'll see what an eclectic bunch of people make up SCRIBE. But we're holding a special place for someone like…you. If you've ever thought about writing, you should be part of this community, a place where you will be encouraged, inspired, challenged and rewarded.

Finally, to my fellow SCRIBE members: Congratulations, you're in print! I pray this is just the first step for you and that you will continue to find your voice as a writer. I also hope that we can publish many more anthologies like this one in the years to come. Right? Write?

Mike Robertson, editor

"Of making many books
there is no end."

— Ecclesiastes 12:12

TABLE OF CONTENTS

WRITER'S BLOCK

Bob Moore

I'm a big fan of Bob Moore. Here's a guy in his eighties who is continuing to find new abilities, new gifts. Shortly after we started the Scribe group, Bob read to us one of his memoir/essays and I was immediately won over by his wit and whimsy. It's fitting that we begin this anthology with his musings on the writer's worst fear.

When ideas fail, words come in very handy. Exactly! I sit at the keyboard, writing word after word, not looking up—just writing. The instructor said, "Just write. Don't edit. Just do it." Keep putting words on paper. So I write. I have no idea what to write about. I think I'll write about not having any ideas. Has that been done before? Probably, but not as reluctantly as *I* will do it. Casey Stengel once said, "If people don't want to come out to the ballpark, nobody's going to stop them". That's how I feel about writing. If I don't have any ideas, nobody's going to stop me.

Wait! I have an idea. It's brilliant! I'll write about it.

What was it?

It's already slipped my mind and it was a sensational idea, too. If only I could think what it was. Calm down. Just wipe off the sweat from your forehead and take it easy. It's not life and death. You have two weeks before you have to read to the class.

Christmas just came 'round again. Does it seem that Christmas comes every other month? Why don't I write about Christmas? That's it! I'll write about Christmas—about the poor family who didn't have any money because the Dad worked for a guy exactly like the louse I used to work for. And the family had a crippled kid who tears at your heartstrings. The turkey gets burned, the miserly louse has a revelation and all turns out well in the end because Congress meets, the

Speaker of the House cries and the welfare check arrives in the mail.

Naaah. It's January already. Nobody wants to hear about Christmas—at least not for another month.

Let's see. Don't just sit here. Think!

Writer's block. I could write about blocks. How the Egyptians piled granite block after granite block on top of each other and built a pyramid. That was smart of them—having the big blocks on the bottom and the little ones on top. Those things are heavy. Besides if they did it the other way around it would probably have fallen over from being too top-heavy. But I can't write about top-heavy pyramids. That's been done to death.

Death! I can write about death. I can't write from experience because I haven't died yet, but I could write about the time the dog died unexpectedly from eating too much wicker. That was the last straw. Poor thing. He loved wicker. We had to hide all the wicker baskets which made it really tough to have a picnic.

That's it. I'll write about picnics. The picnic when I was seven years old and had a life-changing experience when I found out that you could put mayonnaise on a peanut butter and banana sandwich.

No. No one wants to hear me read about peanut butter sandwiches.

I think I'll just call it a day and go have a peanut butter sandwich. The others in the class are really good writers. I just have this gibberish. It's enough to make me want to put the quill back in my goose.

TWO ANGELS

Nancy Bode Bussey

Writing can help us make sense of life's little bumps. It may take awhile, but hindsight can reward the author with a jolt of wisdom. Nancy Bussey found a spiritual lesson which started with a simple argument.

What was about to be our first fight turned into much more.

My husband, Charlie, and I were visiting his Aunt Iris in San Francisco in July and had spent the day sightseeing down at the wharf area. We enjoyed a great boat tour that went around Alcatraz and under the Golden Gate bridge. A very brisk wind coupled with temps in the 50's was invigorating for both of us since we were temporarily escaping the Texas heat which had rocketed into triple digits. Following the tour of the harbor, we walked along Fisherman's Wharf and watched dozens of seals sunning themselves on the wooden boat docks. The slick brown creatures postured and called to one another with curious sounding barks. A few of them slipped into the water for a quick swim and then launched themselves back onto the dock with resounding flops. Hungry, we decided to grab a quick bite to eat before heading back to Charlie's aunt's home. After a very late lunch of shrimp cocktails and crab cakes at a café overlooking the bay, we decided we'd better hurry in order to make it back before dark. We were both new to the city and quickly discovered we had different opinions as to which direction to take.

During our week in San Francisco, we had taken the cable cars up and down the steep hills but we were now walking along the wharf area when we began discussing how to return to Aunt Iris's home on Nob Hill.

"It's two blocks over to our left where we catch the cable car," said Charlie. "I'm sure of it."

"That's not the right direction. It's opposite from where you said." I knew my sense of direction was good and his was horrible but, as a newlywed, I didn't really want to make a big deal about the fact that—in that particular area—my skill was better. And I did know him well enough to know that Charlie was not about to ask for directions. He was a man, after all.

We kept arguing and I was convinced that, if we went his way, we would get totally lost in a strange city. This was in 1971, a pre-cellphone era, so we couldn't call his aunt. By now, we were walking in a questionable neighborhood. Young men were slouched in doorways, smoking and passing back and forth large liquor bottles and regarding us with interest. I felt like we had "Tourist" stamped on our foreheads. We kept walking in the direction Charlie believed was right, but I felt more uneasy and told him he was wrong.

That quick, redheaded temper flared and Charlie's blue eyes narrowed. "O.K. Miss Smarty Pants, you just find your own way and we'll see who gets there first!" He turned his back on me and started walking fast to his own destination.

I stood there for a minute with my face turning hot and felt tears welling up. I tend to cry when I get mad, a trait I find actually annoying and a bit too girly. Then I took a deep breath and told myself to get moving. I'll show him, I thought. I will get there first!

I picked up my pace, which was a bit difficult since I was going up a pretty steep hill.

It was late afternoon and the shadows were lengthening from the buildings that were packed closely against one another. I knew that I could not make it back to where we were staying by nightfall unless I caught the trolley, and I started to sweat even though the temperature was dropping. Some of the buildings looked deserted with broken windows and trash piled around the edges. Shadows were getting longer and darker.

After spending a few days in San Francisco, we had taken quite a few of the trolleys and I was fairly certain I could find the right one. But when I searched my purse I discovered that all I had was a dime and I needed thirty-five cents. This was not good.

I began walking as fast as I could, not wanting to attract attention. A woman, walking alone, with a camera on a shoulder strap, in a shady area of town, presented what might be a pretty easy target. I was madder and madder at Charlie for putting me in this compromising position. And I hoped he was lost! It would serve him right, I fumed, as I continued to climb the hill with my heart racing, as much from fear as from exertion.

As I walked past decrepit buildings and street dogs that were snarling and scrounging for scraps, I noticed an old lady in the doorway of an apartment building. She was watching me and called out, "Miss?"

I approached her cautiously. No more than five feet tall, the lady's grey hair was carefully swept off her face into a graceful bun, topped with a blue fuzzy knitted cap. Her worn sweater was clean as were her saddle Oxfords. Her blue eyes were bright behind her wire-rimmed glasses.

"Would it be too much trouble if you helped me with my groceries?"

It was then I noticed the two grocery sacks at her feet. I looked around and didn't sense anyone about to ambush the two of us so I said, "Certainly." I followed her up one long flight of narrow stairs. There was not an elevator in sight.

When we reached the top of the landing, she turned and said, "Please just leave them by my front door. I can get them from here. It's just that my knees aren't what they used to be. Thank you."

"You are very welcome. I'm glad I was here to help." When she started to reach in her purse—for some change, I guessed—I said, "Oh no, you don't owe me anything."

"It's all right dear," she said with a slight smile. "This is just what you need."

What a curious thing to say, I thought. She pressed some coins into my hand and, in the blink of an eye, she and her two bags had vanished into her apartment.

I opened my palm. Two dimes and a nickel. Twenty-five cents! Just enough to pay for the trolley. I wanted to tell her just how much more she had helped me than I had her, but the door had shut. I felt a sense of peace and calm that dispelled the fear.

I walked confidently and quickly to the trolley stop and, yes, my sense of direction played out just fine. Boarding the trolley and handing over my change, I said a silent prayer of thanks for the presence of an unlikely angel.

But as the city lights starting twinkling and brightening a darkened sky, another thought came to mind.

Was I—unknowing—her angel, too?

LETTERS TO TERRI

Bob Allen

Bob has been a dependable member of Scribe *since the beginning. He always shows up early for our meetings and he's said from the start that he felt the short story was his realm in which to work. In this piece, he's chosen to tell a story from World War II via a set of letters written from a soldier to his girl back home.*

August 18, 1942

Dear Terri,

Sorry I haven't written in so long. In my last letter I told you that we were being shipped out, but I didn't know our destination at that time. Then we were told not to write to anyone until we reached our destination. On August 7, we landed on the island of Guadalcanal. I had never even heard of it before, but they say it is crucial for us to control this island. The Japs had started building an airfield here and we have to take it from them and drive them from the island.

I am assuming the mail censors will block out the name of the island, and other details I give you, but I am going to write them anyway. For the first week after we landed, we were kept busy setting up our base of operations. Resistance from the Japanese has been sparse so far.

I miss you terribly. I think about you all the time and I carry the picture of us that my mom took at our wedding. The other guys and I have been trained to operate in combat conditions, but we have yet to be shot at by the enemy. I think we will operate well as a team and we can carry out our mission, but underneath all that we do and everywhere we go, you are there. I long to talk to you…to hold you. You and I had a couple of years in high school to get to know each other, but I don't think we had enough time before I shipped out. There were so many things we could have done and talked about.

I want us to make up for lost time when I get home.

Sorry this is such a short letter. It took me three days to write it because that is all the time we had. I am looking forward to a letter back from you, but I know it will be at least a month or so before we get mail.

I love you, Terri. I hope this war is over soon so I can come back to you. Write to me and let me know what is going on in your life.

Love, David

August 23, 1942

Dear Terri,

The day after I wrote to you last time, we got into a battle with the Japs. It was a difficult fight, but we won it. I am doing fine, except for being really tired. Combat is a lot different than I had pictured it. It is not as glamorous as the movies make it out to be. People are shooting at us and we have to shoot back. I know I killed some of the enemy, but I don't know how many. I hate to think that we have to kill other people. It is not something I am proud of.

Terri, I hate being here. I want to be with you. Don't get me wrong. I can do my job and I am good at it. These guys I have trained with and now have fought beside are my family. I love them all and when one gets hurt, it is like it happens to my own brother.

We have another enemy now, and it is having a major effect on us. Dysentery. It hit us hard not too long after we landed. I have been sick for three days, but I have to keep going. And the mosquitoes are about the size of B-25's. We are told to not let them bite us. How do we do that? They are everywhere! They say we could get malaria or something.

When they first put us out here in the field, there were not enough meals to go around. We have only had one or two meals a day since we got here. Most of it is C-Rations. Ugh!! Remind me to tell you about them when I get home.

Terri, my heart aches for you. I want to see you, touch you, kiss you, hold you. You mean so much to me. I don't think I can ever tell you how much. I hope you are safe and doing well. Hopefully, this will all be over soon and we can be together again. I think we should talk about having children when I get back. Maybe a little boy that looks like me and a little girl that looks like you. I can already see them in my mind. We will all make a wonderful family. Got to go…we are moving out again.

Love, David

August 28, 1942

Dear Terri,

I have very mixed emotions about what to tell you. Part of it is that I don't want you to worry about me. I have seen so much and experienced so much that I can't talk about yet. Guys I know are getting hurt and killed and it is hard to face. I sometimes worry that I might not make it home to you. I have this deep feeling that in order for this war to end, sacrifices have to be made. I hope I am not one of them.

Something new I have experienced is fear. I hate to tell you that I am afraid. I think all the guys are, but most won't admit it to each other. The fear of being a casualty is always present. When the shooting starts, the feeling becomes almost overwhelming. That is where my Marine Corps training kicks in. The things I have been taught help me make it through the fearful times because my reactions become almost automatic.

Terri, sometimes I am so lonely. Oh sure, I have men all around me and they are all like family. We have been through a lot together. But when I am in the foxhole waiting for some kind of contact with what seems like a faceless enemy, it is just me. It is up to me to kill the enemy before they can kill me. It is ultimately me who has to pull the trigger. I really wish I could be back home. I hate the feeling that I could be all right one minute and the next minute could be dead or wounded. But I know my job and I am determined to do it to the best of my ability.

I'll write to you again when I get the chance.

Love, David

September 2, 1942

My Dearest Terri,

I don't know what day this is. I just guessed and put down a date. We have been in the jungle for about a week or so. For the last two nights, my home has been a crater hole from a mortar shell that exploded during one of our many battles. Once in a while a patrol of Japanese soldiers will stumble on our position and there will be a firefight.

I wish our leaders could be here. Not the generals. They know what it is like. I'm talking about the President and the members of Congress. The emperor of Japan and his staff, whatever they are called. I wish they could experience war from this side instead of from their comfortable rooms. I think there would be a lot fewer wars.

Terri, my heart is so heavy. I lost Johnny Clawson. You remember me talking about him. We met in boot camp and he was probably the best friend I had here. He was always laughing and joking. He had a way of cheering everybody up. I am crying now as I write this. I hate it that he got killed. Last night we were advancing on the enemy lines. He was beside me. We had to go slow and be quiet so the Japs couldn't hear us coming. Suddenly there was a flare lighting up our position and gunfire came from everywhere. Johnny pushed me and I fell to the ground. I heard the sound when the bullet hit him. He didn't say anything…not a word. The sound was like board hitting a wet blanket. Kind of a "whop" sound. I will never, as long as I live, forget that sound. Bullets were flying everywhere. I couldn't tell where to shoot, so I just shot wildly. So did everyone else. Then the flare went out, it was dark again and everyone stopped shooting. I called to Johnny, just in a loud whisper, but somehow I knew he was dead. For two hours there was sporadic gunfire on both sides. We couldn't move. We were pinned down. When it started to get light, we could see bodies in the field around us. That is when I saw Johnny. I crawled over to him, but there was nothing I could do. I am so sad, I don't know what to do. I feel like a part of me died with him. He was the closest thing to a brother I ever had. I am so angry that they would take Johnny from me. I have to make them pay for that. I know that even if I killed them all, it wouldn't bring Johnny back, but somehow, someone needs to pay for his death.

Terri, I have to tell you something that has been bothering me today. While we were on the ship on the way here, Johnny and I got into a discussion about what we thought combat would be like. I suppose all the Marines wondered about that, wondering if they would make it out or be killed or wounded. During the conversation Johnny looked deeply into my eyes. He became very solemn. It kind of scared me at the time. I thought he said, "David, I would die for you".

I was embarrassed and I laughed it off and I changed the subject. Now that he is dead, I am thinking back and wondering whether he said he *would* die for me or he *will* die for me. It gives me chills that he might have known that he was going to die and that by dying he might somehow save me. I wish I could remember exactly what he said.

We have to win this war. If we don't, Johnny and all the others will have died in vain. We can't let that happen. We will keep on until every last one of the enemy is dead.

I love you, Terri. I need you. When I get home, I don't want us to ever part again. We have to live out our lives together and make it a good life. That is the only thing that will make up for Johnny and my other friends dying.

Oh, it is time to pull out again. I will write again when I have a chance.

Love, David

Dear Terri,

I am going to make it!! I know now that somehow Johnny's death has freed me to live. Don't ask me how I know this, but I know it deep down in my heart. It was three days ago when Johnny died. When I woke up this morning, the feeling was overwhelming. Somehow he knew that one of us would die here. Somehow he knew that if he died, I possibly wouldn't. I know, it sounds stupid, but I believe it in my heart. And I feel that Johnny purposely sacrificed himself for me.

If I talked to the company head shrink about this, he would break out the straitjacket and lock me up in a padded cell. So I can't tell anyone else what I am feeling. You are the only one I can trust with this.

They say our operation here is about over and that we are going to be transferred to another island somewhere. But I'm not worried about my life any more. And I know that in time the war will end and I will return to you.

Terri, I think about you all the time. I love you dearly and I can't wait to be with you again. Take care of yourself and I will see you hopefully sooner than later.

Love, David

There Is No End

A SHORT STORY ABOUT THE LIFE OF DAVE

by Stan Lackey

In our deck of SCRIBE writers, Stan Lackey is the Joker. In a previous life, he was a successful "shock jock" with a hugely successful syndicated radio show. A dramatic conversion experience has changed his life, but his sense of humor still marches to the beat of a different accordion. It's too bad you can't hear this story read in his resonant radio voice. How can he talk that way with his tongue in his cheek? The following story is—I think— completely fictional.

If you were to poll the people in the town where Dave lived and died, you would most likely find that there is general surprise that someone would write about his life. Some, if not most, would just come out and ask why you weren't writing a story about Stan, and they would undoubtedly say this next part beaming with pride: "Stan lives in our town, too. Plus, he's still alive!"

But a writer keen on gathering the pertinent data on the life of Dave would persist, and soon discover that Dave was also well-liked and had many friends to boast of himself. Granted, his circle of friends could be drawn inside Stan's circle of friends with a soccer field of space leftover, but soon another astonishing fact emerges: the intensity of fondness for Dave by Dave's friends is nowhere near as intense as the fondness Stan receives from his. Another interesting fact about Dave: everyone who liked Dave also loves Stan but only a small percentage of the people who love Stan even *liked* Dave!

As one would expect, Dave's wife proves to be a fount of information about Dave, and we soon learn that—although she would quickly describe their marriage as a good one—it was not without its share of turbulence. She tells us that at one point Dave had seemed determined for a change and, specifically, had been pondering a change in companions, but Stan had sternly warned Dave that if he forsook his wife then he (Stan) would not fail to step in and marry her. Dave quickly came to realize that if Stan thought his wife that desirable then, clearly, Dave had sorely undervalued her. We are somewhat uncomfortable with the admission that comes next, that many times thereafter, Dave's wife *wished* Dave would have left her so that Stan could honor his promise to marry her. She further tells us that, truth be told, all of the townswomen—every last one of them—secretly yearn for Stan. We take her word on this as that research would be hugely time-consuming and, after all, this is a story about Dave.

After Dave finished high school, lacking the funds for college, he sought employment there in the town. Like most people in town, when out of work he searched out the town's largest employer... Stan. Stan owns nearly three-quarters of the town's shops, factories, clinics, gas stations, restaurants, The Grove—the town's outdoor mall—and all of the businesses that maintain offices in the town's largest building, Stan's Tower Of The Americas, which stands 68 stories tall, whereas the next tallest building in town is five stories.

One would suppose that Stan had inherited this local empire, but surprisingly, this is not the case. Stan began accumulating his massive holdings with but one single enterprise, delivering pizzas. Many customers would actually order a pizza just so Stan would come to their house. This eventually forced the pizza owner to offer his customers just Stan *without* a pizza, charging them eight dollars for a twelve-minute conversation with Stan.

But back to Dave.

Dave eventually became an executive at K-STAN, the town's TV station. Stan became so trusting of Dave that when he (Stan) left town to busy himself with either his NFL franchise or his Major League Baseball concern, he would leave Dave in charge at the station. When Dave entered what the townsfolk call his "cocaine years," Stan even provided paid leave for Dave to receive treatment at Stan's Hand, his 400-acre rehab facility in Palm Springs.

When Dave was better he offered Stan his resignation, but Stan would not hear of it. Because he was so proud of Dave's recovery, Stan invited Dave to join him in Buenos Aires where he (Stan) was to be a celebrity judge at the Miss Universe pageant. To Dave's even greater surprise, Stan asked Dave to be his best man at his marriage to Miss Singapore later that year.

For many months and years after, Dave's life was filled with happiness and joy, even though that joy mostly consisted of the reflected happiness and joy from Stan's life. When a heart attack claimed his (Dave's) life, Stan spoke at Dave's funeral. Stan's tribute was so moving that afterward many others asked Stan to speak at their funerals, too. Stan, of course, agreed and many have openly spoken of their desire to die just so Stan could speak on their behalf.

Since Dave's death, Stan and his wife, the former Miss Singapore, have become a second family for Dave's three sons, Stanley, Stanton and Stanford, and his daughter Castandra. Today, Stanley works as an executive at StanLand, the world's largest self-contained amusement park, which features over twenty hotels and resorts within the park itself. Stanton manages GrandStan, the largest domed stadium on earth and the permanent site of the Super Bowl beginning in 2012. Castandra oversees UnderStan, the largest gold mine operation in the history of the planet. Stanton, however, decided to follow in his father's footsteps and is currently in Palm Springs "recovering" at Stan's Hand.

So, as you can see, what at first appeared to be an uneventful life (Dave's) has proven to be one filled with interesting peaks and tragic valleys. And though Dave didn't live long enough to see his friend Stan become the first private citizen to walk on the moon or to kill the Antichrist, he still had a full and meaningful life. Rest—at Stan's Remembrance Gardens—in peace, Dave.

HOOD ORNAMENT

Lauren Kinzie

Lauren once asked me to evaluate one of her poems and I had to tell her that I didn't feel all that qualified. Poetry has never been easy for me to understand well enough to make informed judgment. But I looked at her work and began to see a skillful use of language that even I could notice and appreciate. Several of her poems appear in this volume. And I think I'm starting to get it.

I am not your hood ornament,

advertising money and power,

and providing compensations

for Nature's oversights.

I'm not your Barbie,

a perfect, ridiculous fantasy.

I am not an appliance

You can turn "off,"

and toss back in the closet,

with all the broken toys and

headless Barbies.

Not your cuff-links, bling,

or party accessory.

Definitely not your Viagra—

transporting you back to a bygone and better-forgotten era...

I'm not "two tickets to paradise"

or an escape from

the rat race,

your ex,

or your mama.

Not the mothership to your barnacle.

I am not a receptacle

for

Blame,

Shame,

Angst,

Or failures.

I am not redemption in a long, white dress

or a cheat- sheet to some kind of test.

I am not the GOAL!

or prey

to capture, control or take away.

I am not your brain or your conscience

or a second chance at infancy.

Don't sign me up!

I'm not your trophy or your crew.

I am not Joan of Arc

or St. Jude.

Treatment of martyrs has historically been pretty rude.

I'm not your last chance at anything.

So, stop staring at me,

if you are determined not to see.

THE PRODIGAL'S ODYSSEY

Peter A. Hubbard

Like many of us, Peter Hubbard loves the parable of the Prodigal Son. Unlike the rest of us, however, he took it upon himself to explore that story in much greater detail, expanding it to novel-length. In this excerpt, we learn much more about the Prodigal's life before he hit bottom and decided to make the long trek homeward.

Good morning, Theophilus, and thank you for coming on such short notice. I value your skills as a scribe, and trust you to make an accurate report. Unfortunately, my fever is not responding to the doctor's herbs, so I believe my time has come. Sit here next to me so you can begin writing out my last will and testament.

No, I have no regrets. I have lived a very full life. Now that I've reached the venerable age of 77 and no longer have my health, I'm eager to join my ancestors who have gone on before me. But before discussing the division of my earthly goods, I want to impart some very important details, known only to a few outside our community.

I want everyone to know that Jesus' parable of the Prodigal Son was not simply an illustration of our Heavenly Father's unconditional love—it was a piece of *my* story. It was much more than a parable. It actually happened.

I met Jesus on one of his many visits to Cesearea. He came to our estate when I was in my late 30's, and that's when I came to understand he was the Messiah. Jesus wanted to use my story of restoration because he knew it would help others come to know our Heavenly Father.

Those familiar with the parable know me as an adventuresome youth, intent on getting my inheritance early, leaving home and experiencing everything the Roman Empire and Mediterranean world had to offer—which I did. But no one knows the full story of my Odyssey, or exactly what happened after my repentant return. Few know exactly why I left, what led to my eventual return, and what happened after the "welcome home" feast.

Growing up, my name was not Xavier. My parents prophetically named me Phillip, which means "lover of horses." They could not possibly have known the important role horses would play later in my life, when I became a successful charioteer during my selfish odyssey.

The name truly fit, because even at birth I was high-spirited. Growing up, I constantly sought out excitement and adventure, driven by an innate sense of curiosity. As a youth I could find no better companion for exploration and adventure than a good horse, capable of swiftly transporting me wherever I wished to go.

My older brother was named Hiram, which means "exalted brother." And that's precisely what he was. He was preferred over me by my father and family members—indeed, everyone on the estate.

As the first-born son and primary heir, Hiram had it made! What angered me most was that he didn't have to earn a thing. His status was not based on any virtue in his character, any personal skill or some extraordinary or heroic accomplishment. He simply had the stinking good luck to be born male—and born first.

My memories as "second son" are painful. I felt excluded, overlooked, or simply forgotten—shuffled off to household servants and tutors—rather than being nurtured and cared for by my father, Abraham. Deep in my bones, I never felt like a cherished son. Instead, I saw myself as an irritation—an afterthought. I might as well have been an orphan.

Things were a bit better before my baby sister, Susannah died. She was a delight. I thoroughly enjoyed playing games with her and being "big brother." Hiram couldn't be bothered. More important duties demanded his attention. He was being groomed to oversee the orchards, vineyards and livestock on the estate as early as age twelve. He was learning how to supervise field workers and went almost everywhere with our Father. They were inseparable.

Naturally, my mother Hannah was heartbroken when Susannah died. So was I. She was as frail and fragile as the petals on the spring flowers. Since she bruised easily when she fell down, or bumped herself while playing, Mother and I were very protective. I always made sure she didn't stray off by herself.

Sadly, Susannah was no match for the plague that took her when she was only seven. Mother tried in vain to nurse her back to health. The plague invaded her lungs, and simply squeezed the living breath out of her. Making matters worse, the plague claimed my mother's life five months later.

I was devastated. The only two people in my family to whom I felt connected were gone. And I wanted to be gone, too. But I didn't want to join them in death … I wanted to *live*!

Yes, I probably held my father responsible—for being so obsessed with business, and not caring enough about his family. It seemed like he was always working, and never around when I needed to talk with him. We lived on a large trading estate, near the seaside port of Cesearea, supplying the Roman army and the ruling bureaucracy with large quantities of food, clothing, furniture and tools. We also exported goods to Asia, Greece and Italy, even as far away as Carthage and Spain.

If he wasn't ensuring that trade agreements were properly negotiated, contracts signed, and shipping arrangements made, he was busy administering activities on our bustling estate. It seemed there were always disputes between servants to settle, or a myriad other administrative duties more important than me, requiring his precious time.

I wanted to be free of my father's indifference … and I wanted it now! I yearned to travel those Roman roads I'd heard so much about, to the very edges of the Empire and beyond. I wanted to see and experience everything life had to offer.

So I began making plans to achieve that freedom. I demanded that my father hand over my inheritance early, even though doing so would bring shame on him and go against all the social norms of my day. I didn't care.

It took time to collect all the assets; at least two or three months passed before my father completed all the deals. Orchards, and vineyards, olive groves and nut and fig trees that would have been mine were leased to other landowners, as were fields of barley and wheat. Cattle, sheep, goats and horses were sold and monies collected. When it was all done, I had ten talents of gold and lines of credit with merchants all across the Roman Empire worth ten more. It would have taken the average laborer over thirty years to accumulate the wealth I inherited.

When I left, I also took along a traveling companion, named Daniel. We had grown up together on the estate. His father was a doctor, the physician who worked with herbs and medicines, providing various healing tonics and ointments.

Our ultimate destination was Rome, of course, but we took our sweet time getting there. We arrived six months later, after stopping at various cities in Asia and Greece to meet the trading merchants with whom my father had made the financial arrangements.

Shortly after arriving in Rome, Daniel and I purchased a large, roomy villa on the outskirts, already finely furnished. It had a separate servant's quarters, plus a stable for the horses I would soon acquire.

Naturally, Daniel and I began indulging in all the pleasures Rome had to offer. We quickly made friends with the other affluent young Romans. Some we met at the baths, others at the theatre, as well as the Coliseum, at Circus Maximus, and various festivals. We became quite popular with our new friends, thanks to the lavish parties we threw. There was always plenty of great food, wine—and loose women. Our taste in young women tended toward those with artistic skills. We enjoyed meeting them at the bazaars where they sold their crafted jewelry, leather goods, or fine woven garments made from exotic imported cloth.

But our enjoyment of pleasures of the flesh didn't stop there. Like other wealthy young Romans, we acquired slaves. We bought five slaves, two younger women, two older women and a manservant to help tend the horses and the grounds. The women did our cooking, baking, cleaning, and serving party guests. They also did other things, like satisfying our carnal desires. We also enjoyed the intimate company of exotic prostitutes brought to Rome from the four corners of the empire.

Daniel and I also enjoyed other amusements, including the theatre, and befriended several actors, dancers, musicians and writers. Daniel was a natural on stage, and soon joined a touring acting troupe.

But being a horse-lover, I was drawn more to Circus Maximus and the chariot races held there almost weekly. Not only were the horses fabulous to watch, so were the skilled charioteers. And the racing chariots were also a marvel, sleek and swift, crafted of the finest and lightest woods and canvas.

Naturally, racing strategies resulted in crashes, often resulting in debilitating or fatal injuries to men and horses alike. The Circus Maximus provided an awesome spectacle, with 100,000 screaming race fans, rooting for either the White, Red, Blue or Green teams.

At my very first race, I decided that *this* was what I was born to do. Since I had money then—and lots of it—it wasn't too difficult to arrange. Even though most drivers were either slaves or freedmen, I was able to become a winning charioteer, an *aurigae*, since I was a "foreigner," not a citizen.

I soon obtained my own horses, and was able to "buy in," joining the Red Team. Over a period of about nine months, I was trained in the high-stakes art of chariot racing by one of the very best drivers in the entire empire—Scorpus—who had won well over a thousand races. In the back of my mind I knew I was wagering with my life, since the chances of injury or death were very high. But I didn't care. I was young and daring, eager for adventure and possible fame.

So it was settled. I was off to the races…literally! At that point, Daniel and I sold our villa and parted ways. He left to pursue the applause of the theatres, while I was pursued the thundering applause of the Circus Maximus, and other racetracks across the empire.

Thanks to my excellent horsemanship, over the next five years I became a fairly successful charioteer traveling the length and breadth of the Roman Empire. I managed to win over 250 races, mostly for the Red Team, and earned over 500,000 sestertii. The monetary winnings were enormous, and allowed me to travel the Empire and maintain the lifestyle to which I'd grown accustomed. Of course, that included lots of victory parties, awash with wine, women and song.

But it all came to a quick and painful end, during a race in Toledo, Spain. While I had been involved in dramatic crashes before that, I had always managed to walk away with only minor cuts and bruises. But that day was different.

My memories are most vivid. There must have been at least 40,000 screaming, cursing, sweating fans, all intent on exercising their vocal chords under the relentless Spanish sun. Adding to the deafening roar was the shrill neighing of a hundred equally sweaty horses, straining at their stall doors, eager to be underway. The auditory assault on my eardrums was equally matched by the offensive stench wafting toward my nostrils

Eleven preliminary heats determined the finalists for the Winner's Race at the Toledo Circus that steamy July day. I had easily won my early heat, as my sleek quadriga—a custom-made four-horse chariot—outpaced those driven by local Spaniards by at least four lengths. In addition to the cheers of the crowd, the winner would receive 20,000 sestertii.

Weeks without rain had turned the dusty track harder than stone. And despite the efforts of track stewards, who brought in dozens of wagons loaded with sand to make the surface race ready, the all-day pounding by chariot wheels and horse's hooves had opened small cracks in the earth, which by day's end had turned into gaping ruts.

While I'd raced on rough courses before, none compared to the condition of the Toledo track that day. At the blare of the starting horn I did my best to steer my steeds around the worst of them, and prayed the other drivers would not force me off my intended course. But fate had other ideas. The race was going well, with me in either first or second place during the first six laps.

Heading around the final turn into the seventh and final lap, I was in second, and aiming inside the leader to retake first place before the finish. But I never made it. The horses pulling the Green chariot, coming up from behind, nudged my wheels into one of the deepest ruts on the track, where it stuck fast. As my chariot was breaking apart, my momentum hurled me skyward before gravity slammed me back to earth. I remember the stabbing pain as I hit the ground. Then everything went black.

Days later, when I finally awoke, I learned my body had been trampled by at least three teams of horses, who kicked my bruised and battered frame into the center wall, the spina, where I lay for several minutes before the doctors could retrieve me. Fortunately, some of the best doctors in Spain were on hand that day, and able to stop the bleeding and re-set my broken bones.

While both legs had been broken, I could still walk ... but would never race again. From hitting my head on the concrete wall, my vision was permanently blurred. My left arm was badly hurt, too, resulting in very limited range of motion.

I needed many months to fully recover. My income now gone, the payments for lodging and for doctors and nurses quickly drained what remained of my wealth. A shadow of my former self—physically as well as financially—I recognized that my future appeared bleak. I was alive, but just barely. The only "career option" still open to me was menial labor. And the only job I could find in that drought-stricken land was tending swine.

I wanted to go home, but I couldn't ... or could I? What God seemed to tell me in those dark gray moments was this: "Remember what I did for Moses and the children of Israel as they faced the Red Sea? If you humble yourself, I can make a way where there is no way."

What happened next, you already know, being familiar with Christ's parable. I made it back home. What you don't know, however, is what happened after the giant welcome home party. I'm very eager to relate to you everything else that happened between my brother and me, and how I eventually become lord of the estate. It was all very interesting.

However, my dear Theophilus, my energy is waning. Why don't you come back tomorrow, and we'll pick up the story from there.

ALL WITH REASON

Salli Smith

One of the best things about poetry is how every reader can draw his or her own meaning from the wordcraft provided by the poet. Salli Smith provides this work, full of possible meanings for each of us to discover. I know what it says to me; what about you?

There was nothing overhead…

Except moss,

Hanging from the trees without reason.

The night was pitch-black

And the wind was non-existent,

Where spirits soar and wander.

A mind within itself,

Where reality truly lies.

Wooded forest surrounding, enclosing,

Applying pressure from inside.

A force too great to control?

Maybe, for the decision is given to each.

Most too frightened to reach in

Behind the curtain of life.

Safe and sound, more appealing.

Shadows are tempting though…

Bringing curiosity to the soul,

Intriguing the brain and heart simultaneously.

Is this a desire of life perhaps,

And destination, simply a state of mind?

Possibly containing solitude

But not peace,

For that only comes after death.

So at present, life demands thought and imagination.

Answers are given by forces lurking in the universe.

It costs though, in one way or another…

Almost as if intelligence is earned.

Good and evil appear equal,

Goodness will reign victorious.

Capable of survival in this constant darkness,

Where even twilight is only a dream?

I look up to the heavens for assistance.

One day, I know all of this ebony surrounding will eventually pass.

But for now, I experience and wait in this forest of life,

With nothing existing except moss overhead…

MY FEAR OF FLYING MONKEYS

By Kathy Souther

Is there a person alive today whose life has not been touched by the grim specter of cancer? It comes as no surprise that two of our Scribe authors submitted pieces concerning their own battles with this way-too-prevalent disease. Kathy Souther remembers it well, though it's been over a decade since she heard that dreaded diagnosis.

FEAR.

This word can stand alone to conjure up a response, but often it's teamed up with adjectives like "heart-stopping, riveting, gripping, and paralyzing." My earliest memories of feeling this emotion came from the annual showing of *The Wizard of Oz* in the 1960's. Watching the black and white version of an ominous tornado descending upon the unsuspecting Kansas farm and whirling Dorothy away from her family was enough to give me recurrent nightmares. Not to mention the pure terror felt in watching those grotesque flying monkeys levitating in flight formation on a gruesome mission to capture Dorothy and Toto. That was classic fear!

If you Google "What is fear?" there are 265,000,000 results from the search engine. Wikipedia simply defines Fear as "a distressing emotion induced by a perceived threat". I believe "perceived" is the operative word in this definition and therefore explains my survival from countless fear-rendering experiences in my life thus far. Everyone knows that evil flying monkeys aren't real…right?

There aren't many flying monkeys looming around in adulthood, yet I've encountered situations that elicit the same emotional responses as those sweet childhood fears. The stakes were much higher in my grown-up version of distress; in particular, one such event came about in the form of a cancer diagnosis.

It was Easter week in 2001. Fear has a way of embedding even small details of an experience vividly so that they may be recalled for many years to come.

Drip…drip…drip… A distant thrumming noise is tapping out a cadence as I sit with my brother, knee to knee, eye to eye, in front of me. He is working to come up with yet another amusing story to entertain me from our family anecdotal arsenal, and he does not fail this time. I am comforted and enjoy the welcome alternative of laughter to other dark emotions that I am feeling. His worried eyes move away from me, to look at the to-go cup of iced tea by my side and very calmly he says, "Looks like we have a problem." Drip…drip…drip… I turn to follow where his eyes are now looking, and see that my IV has sprung a leak, and instead of making its way down the highway of tubing into my body, has now taken a detour to gently, slowly drip into my iced tea glass.

It also catches the nurse's attention immediately. She orders everyone to stand back and asks if anyone had come in contact with the leak. She calls for another nurse and together they pull out a HAZMAT collection kit, following strict procedure for a spill of hazardous chemicals. They cover themselves head to foot with gloves, gowns and masks and wave away those surrounding me. Everyone pulls away—a bit embarrassed—as if to wonder, what exactly is the Miss Manners protocol for this? How can we show our love and support yet at the same time, disregard our fear of the toxic chemical leak? I am spinning in fear as I think that this is ME! I'm the one soaking in these tiny droplets that are supposedly saving me, yet are governed by HAZMAT guidelines.

This moment is one of countless times in my cancer journey that I still, after ten years can vividly recall. I had just celebrated my forty-third birthday, and had accepted a fantastic career opportunity in the high tech industry. Life was in a really good place for the first time in quite a while, so naturally God and the wisdom of the universe decided to chart an alternate route.

From the moment I received the diagnosis, I couldn't begin to fathom the amazing year ahead of me. A verdict of cancer and the word "amazing" would not typically be in proximity to one another in a sentence; but I choose the word "amazing" because it's the word I think of when I recall the sum total of what happened during this time. In this year, in the face of so much fear, I gained insights about myself and what I was made of. I also received an endless supply of love from my family and friends, and discovered how faith can grow in leaps and bounds when your mortality is examined and on the line. Fear is faith's gymnasium. Yep, "amazing" is what comes to mind as I think about that year, but, of course, only now from the safe vantage point of a decade gone by.

I had noticed a strange swelling in my left thigh and had made an appointment with my doctor to discuss it. She seemed puzzled and ordered a series of tests, including my soon-to-be-favorite, the MRI. The machine, after about an hour's worth of scary whirling, knocking and banging, brought forth images of a very large tumor in the back part of my thigh.

I would soon learn that the tumor had a name, liposarcoma, which makes up a very small percentage of all cancers. It actually ranks in the category of a "rare disease," which places me in the unique status of being a "cancer snob." It also carries with it a 50% chance of recurrence which made the next several years especially faith-inspiring. Chances for any type of recurrence are extremely slim once the five-year anniversary mark successfully passes. However, without a crystal ball to see my healthy future, I was faced with frightening survival odds that could play out in a single coin toss.

I was heading toward middle age and now felt like a child who was frightened beyond my worst nightmares. I would've sincerely welcomed a bunch of flying monkeys to cart me away from what I now was facing.

Because the cancer was so rare, I was told it had to be treated at large cancer institute such as MD Anderson Cancer Center in Houston. I was assigned to an incredible doctor who was nationally known for making strong progress in this form of cancer. From the start, she never dispensed "survival rates" but instead gave me lots of encouragement, told me to eat broccoli and try yoga. With all the uncertainty that cancer brings, what I know for sure is that positive thinking, humor, and prayer power were my talisman on this journey. They also helped to wipe out the futility of my fear.

As I headed for my first appointment, on the drive to Houston from Austin, it felt surreal to think about my circumstances and how my life had been completely derailed. Of the many emotions I was feeling during that time, my emotion of fear was rising to unprecedented proportions as I realized that the perception of a threat (flying monkeys) was now replaced by the reality of a threat (cancer morbidity rates). Up until this point, my definition of fear was the feeling I had when I saw a spider, rode on a roller coaster or watched a movie involving Hannibal Lecter. I had never confronted a legitimate fear of losing my life. Like a great monster of epic proportions, I had to learn how to manage this fear and keep it at bay. I began to look to God for signs, which—once I actually began looking—I found frequently. My first major "God wink" was along the drive to Houston. Over an open field I saw the magical beauty of a double rainbow and I couldn't help but believe it was sent from God to say all would be okay. My next assurance came as I nervously entered the cancer-fighting metropolis of MD Anderson: the gleaming Starbucks logo, a beacon of familiarity in the middle of a very foreign and scary world. It was difficult to imagine myself as a patient in this monstrosity of a cancer hospital, and yet here I was, grande Café Latte in hand, with few alternatives. MD Anderson is known as one of the worlds's most recognized and leading cancer institutes…and they don't take this mission lightly. They work to cure over 100,000 patients who are seen annually, treating every kind of cancer imaginable, and probably some that are beyond imagination. They proudly boast that 10 languages are spoken here and soon it's easy to observe that cancer knows no boundaries and speaks all languages. As I moved thru the labyrinth of buildings, I saw a multitude of bald heads walking and wheeling through the halls, and above all, a sea of brave and determined patients and caregivers who come from every conceivable geography and background. I, along with family and friends, was continuously daunted by the sensory overload of this place. There is a feeling of palpable fear and anxiety that buzzes in the air, yet underlying it is a strong spirit of commonality as everyone is joined together in one place to fight a common cause: to end cancer in all its ugly shapes, forms and stages. Once I was able to rise and reign above the fear, I knew that the mere strength in numbers around me—the fellow patients, the amazing doctors, the nurses whom many believe are God's angels on earth—would lend a vast source of strength to draw from. And last, but far from least, my faith in God's love. In my heart, and soon-to-be-bald head, the only way I would remotely survive this dark time, was truly to let go and lean into God for all the untapped strength and peace that only He can offer. This became my mantra, and countless blessings unfolded.

Through six intensive chemotherapy treatments, five weeks of radiation that also included "chemo lite" and the grand finale of a four hour surgery, I have many moments of true grit and courage to draw from. One time that especially comes to mind was during my final weeks of radiation therapy. In an appointment with my surgeon, she informed me there was a strong possibility I would have to wear a brace on my leg going forward. I had been convinced that after all the months of treatment, once it was all behind me, I would bear no outwardly visible results of this disease.

I went to my following radiation treatment and lay on the table waiting to be zapped. My spirit had already been zapped.

The radiation technician always had great music filling the room with artists like Eric Clapton which helped to provide a small dose of normalcy. As I lay waiting for the humming of the equipment and the music to begin, my thoughts were of how I had reached the bottom of a long coast downhill. Oddly, the music from German composer George Frideric Handel's 'Messiah' began to play. My optimistic faith had hit a wall, and now the most majestic music and lyrics came soaring through the air. At the precise moment I needed it most, the words "And He shall reign forever and ever!" reminded me that the amazing promise of eternal life is like a bucket of water dousing fear of physical harm, or ultimate death. Just like my childhood fears of fictitious wicked witches and monkeys, my adult fears of mortality had been eased.

I felt redeemed as I left the room. Ironically, there was a message on my cell phone waiting from my surgeon, who called to let me know she had just presented my case to her colleagues and they all were in agreement that the tumor could be removed without causing the damage which would require a leg brace. Hallelujah. Begone, you flying monkeys!

Ten years have passed since this difficult yet amazing year which was steeped in fear. Like Dorothy, I was returned back to the sweet routine of life with nothing much changed…and yet *everything* changed. The year had not been about the medieval torturous process of fighting cancer and experiencing the fragility of my mortality, all which were eventful on their own standing. This year was about the absolutely awe inspiring power of love; the amount of love that poured to me from family, friends and oftentimes mere strangers is something that made the year one of the most significant of my life thus far.

It was about gaining a connection to God I had never experienced before. I learned that when you find yourself at the lowest possible point, Handel's Messiah is one note away from pouring down on you and validating the fact that God has given us the promise of eternal life, and His great love shines in the faces of fellow human beings everywhere. We only have to seek it. When you're chased by fear in all its ugly forms, such as cancer—or even flying monkeys—the seeking part becomes easy.

MOONLIGHT MEMORIES

Lori Garrigus

In this poem, Lori Garrigus explores the longing feeling of a lost love. It's an experience most of us can relate to, when that one special someone is no longer here, but so many traces and memories remain.

The moon a sliver in an indigo sky,
touched by a silvery star,
brought your face into the
soft shadows of my mind.
Your face bathed in moonlight
as you turned to go
one last time as the dawn
stilled our voices.
In the mist of the morning,
I felt the vapor trail of dreams
you would leave in your wake.
I would miss your kiss
and your caress,
but most of all your poetry –
winsome words of passion
with profound elegance
that made my soul soar

above the pain and loneliness.
As I watched you leave in the
pink gold rays of sunrise,
I tried to memorize you,
to remember every nuance
of your being,
to preserve a little of the
power of your presence.
All these years later,
I can still see your face
and feel your heart beat
in the darkness of a predawn sky.

REUNION

Bob Moore

Should you attend your high school reunion? How bad could it be? Bob Moore knows.

The Holiday Inn selected by the reunion committee was somewhat dated and the green paint job had seen better days. It occurred to me as we drove into the entrance portico that it was probably going to be that way for the Class of '55, fifty years after graduation. I nervously checked my appearance in the rear view mirror, reassuring myself that I did not seem too dated or shopworn as well.

There was no welcoming sign for the Class of '55 in the lobby and no one familiar in sight. One gentleman sitting in an overstuffed chair looked to be about my age. Was he a classmate? If so, he certainly had not weathered the years well. Should I speak to him or just be nonchalant and proceed to our room? I chose the latter. I'll see him later…if he is one of us.

The teenager—at this age, everyone looks like a teenager—showed no emotion whatsoever that I had finally returned to the site of my own teenage memories. I felt like someone, anyone, should be shouting, "Hey, Bob, it's so great to see you." No one did.

For the day's agenda, in the cabinet with the glass door, it said, "Henry Clay H.S Reunion, 7:00 p.m., Bluegrass Room." The unmoved teenager gave me our key and we proceeded to room 307. The window above the rattling air conditioner overlooked the parking lot and there was no bluegrass in sight, only a few parked cars and a bored doorman standing just outside the portico; not an auspicious beginning.

I'm just nervous. That's my problem. Will I recognize anyone after 50 years? Will they recognize me? If not, will they at least remember me? Suppose no one even remembers that I was in the class. Fifty years is a long time. What was the name of our geometry teacher? Who was the kid who played drums in the band and was killed in a car accident? If I meet Mary Saunders, how will I know her? She undoubtedly has a married name by now. Will Tom Price be here? It will be fun to see him after all these years.

It's time to get ready: shower, shave, best suit, new tie, shined shoes. I look in the mirror. "You don't look like you could be going to a fiftieth reunion. That would make you almost seventy years old. You certainly don't look seventy." Sometimes it's necessary to pump up one's self-confidence.

Seven p.m. – the hour of confrontation. The all-female welcoming committee at the name tag table reminded me of three crows sitting on a fence. Who are these people? They obviously had no idea who I was until I filled out my name tag. Even then, there was no elated greeting, just "Sit anywhere you like." That's a relief. I'll mingle and read name tags until I find someone I know. There's Arthur Lieberman, the brainiest kid in the class. I nod and say "Hi." No response. Well, he never spoke to me in school either.

Just then someone tapped me on the shoulder. "Bob Moore, how are you?" I wheeled around and tried to read the name tag without seeming obvious.

"I'm great!" (Who is this? They should make name tags larger.) "Oh, Herman! It's great to see you, too." I had no idea who Herman Sharp was but he obviously knew me.

"Come sit at our table. We'll catch up on old times." This is really going to be embarrassing. I can't remember a single old time with Herman. Where is Tom Price when I need him?

It turns out that Herman and I had been on the football team together but since he was first string and I was a lowly sub, we rarely interacted on or off the field. Besides Herman and his wife, there were two other couples at the table who, as far as I knew, might as well have gone to school on Mars. However, now was my chance to ply Herman with questions about our schoolmates.

"Patsy McGruder was my almost-girlfriend. Whatever became of her?" I ventured.

"She died in Florida, I believe," said Herman.

"Do you remember Tommy Garrison?"

"Sure I do. The last I heard of him, he was an alcoholic and living on the street."

"How about John Heaton?"

"John became a preacher and ran off with the wife of one of his parishioners. Someone said he was living in Indiana."

I kept looking around the now half-filled room for someone—anyone—who might be familiar. Ah-hah! "Is that Betty Wilkinson?"

"Nope. That's Betty over there" and he pointed to one of the crows.

Desperation was setting in. My worst fears were coming true. I knew no one and no one knew me, except for Herman, of course. I could tell he was beginning to have second thoughts about inviting us to sit at his table.

Becoming more desperate by the minute, I thought I would give it another try. "So, Herman, tell me what you've been doing all these years."

"Well, there's really not that much to tell. After I got my law degree from Yale, I served as Assistant Director for the Peace Corps in Africa and later became a consultant to both Nixon and Johnson in urban affairs. After I retired from public service I devoted most of my time to my foundation. You know how dull foundation work can be at times."

I nodded in agreement. Our house in Fresno once had a crack in the foundation and I knew exactly where he was coming from.

But the subject didn't seem worth pursuing and I returned to my old standbys: "Do you ever hear from Tom Price or Sylvia Mayer?" I wasn't the only one who was becoming desperate; Herman had that disgusted look about him.

"Unfortunately both have passed away. Sylvia was quite a knockout as the drum majorette. Do you remember how she used to prance in front of the band?"

Suddenly one of my teenage fantasies came rushing back. It wasn't my only teenage fantasy, of course, but it was one of the better ones.

After drifting off briefly and being poked in the ribs by Phyllis, I decided that probably I should ask her to dance. Billy McGinnis was in front of the band playing his clarinet. Billy was locally famous for his clarinet solos even back then and I could see that fifty years of practice had served him well. He had "Stardust" down pat, playing it even better than he had in 1955. Pete Fountain would be so proud. Phyllis and I did our thing on the dance floor, dips and all, and out of the corner of my eye I could tell that the three old crows were watching admiringly. After the chicken and peas and the cake baked in the shape of the old high school building, it was time for Arthur Lieberman's speech. But first he was introduced by Patti Perrone who gushed for twenty minutes about all of Arthur's accomplishments since leaving Henry Clay. She went on and on about how he was the financier for Steven Spielberg and other such irrelevancies and I thought she would never stop. Arthur, to his credit, spent no time at all talking about Spielberg but he did let us in on some fascinating tidbits about Bob Hope's mansion in Palm Springs. He also mentioned in passing that he and Herman had occasionally collaborated on economic missions in Europe. This all took place at about the same time I was learning to be a sales rep in Fresno. It was an exciting time to be alive.

After two more interminable speeches by people I thought would never make it past junior college it was time to call it a night. "We'll see you for breakfast in the morning," Herman said. Phyllis peered at me as if she were reading my mind. Check out time was eleven.

We were out of there by nine-thirty.

ANIMAL LEGENDRY

Glenda Rhyne

Writers are often asked where they get the ideas for their stories. As Glenda Rhyne shows us, ideas are everywhere; sometimes they stroll right past us, trailing mystery, symbolism and unexplained emotions behind them.

I moved into a subdivision named Davenport Ranch in Austin, Texas, in March of 1984. It is a pleasant neighborhood in the hill country directly west of downtown Austin, rather Mediterranean-looking in the way that large houses extend out over each other from small lots on the hillsides. I placed my desk in the corner of our spacious bedroom in such a way that I looked out over the narrow valley running north and south in front of our home, which faced east from its perch halfway up a high hill.

The land on which I now lived had indeed been a ranch, one which they say served as a gathering place for old-time Democrats in Texas. But we new folks from Minnesota and California and high-tech havens elsewhere were moving in, and the subdivision streets, all named for famous racehorses, were in the constant disarray of construction, moving vans, and For Sale signs. When the dust finally settled and the South of the Border music went home with the last worker's pick-up, however, I could enjoy the late afternoon view from my desk window in peace.

Perhaps it was late summer when I first noticed a solitary border collie on the street below. I saw him in the evenings when I had time to study him, and I would sometimes drive by him on our street in the mornings. I suppose I was struck by the fact that he walked alone, but as if controlled by a leash. A leash law was more or less in effect in our neighborhood, so nearly every canine that walked down our street had a person attached. There were times when a couple of teenaged pups might make a dash about the yards…but taking one's self for a walk, as this dog was doing, caught my imagination. During the first months that I idly noted his comings and goings, always very disciplined and punctual—mid-morning and late afternoon—he looked about as well-kept as the other dogs that were paraded by. When that first winter set in, however, I recognized that the dog was not going home to someone who fed him and brushed his fur.

I finally asked Marty, a neighbor who walked her Lab on the same route, if she knew anything about the dog. "No," she replied. "The security people think that perhaps his owners once lived here and moved away…but he's kept up appearances for so long that they don't have the heart to take him in. He never bothers anyone, not even a trash can."

For nearly five years that solitary animal walked our street twice a day. Day by day, month after month, stretching into years, the animal took the same route, once in mid-morning and then again in the late afternoon. I have sat inside on hundred degree summer days when the glare alone forbade my leaving the house, only to catch sight of the thickly coated collie scorching his feet to take his daily constitutionals. Each year his head hung down further, and his coat became more and more matted. Where he slept or kept himself when he was not walking, none of us learned nor seemed inclined to discover. There was something terribly dignified and private in his dogged determination to make his rounds. If offered food, he stopped and watched our ministrations, but he did not tarry long, and he never ate in our presence. Sometimes the food would be gone the next day, but whether he or the ever-present raccoons devoured it, we never knew for sure. He was not afraid or antagonistic; he was just disinterested, as if we were silly people who did not matter. We were not the right people.

It is amazing, as I look back, that none of us did anything about him. I was not a dog person, so I suppose I left him to those who were. And one or two I know did offer food, questions, a few calls to the Davenport Office, and even concerned conversation with him. But there was something so respectable in his steadfastness that I think we all felt protective of that. He displayed a fortitude, a courage, that shamed us; there was never talk of catching or caging him, of owning him. It was obvious that he belonged to himself and whoever it was who had claimed his allegiance long before. To offer our kind of help seemed, finally, trite; his real needs we could not address, for they ran too deep.

His intimidating aloofness diminished into forlorn as the years passed. His coat slowly disintegrated into motley clumps and his eyesight failed, so that he barely turned his head in acknowledgement of sound or movement. His sore feet faltered, occasionally allowing the front of his forepaw to slide along the pavement as he unbent the first joint to take his next step. The last time I recall actually looking at him (he had ceased to be something one noted in particular, being taken for granted in the landscape), I was driving home from the grocery store. It was a gray, late afternoon. On his now shortened round, he had stopped in front of our house to hang his head, swaying a bit into the cold as if to catch his breath…or to remember something. I came to a stop in awe of him, of the motivation inside him. My attention only prompted his head to rise and his walk to resume.

I may have had occasion to see him many times after that, but I'm not sure. I just realized one day out of the clear blue that the dog no longer walked our street. I had no idea how long it had been since he limped past my window and around the circle in front of Sarah's house and back again. Acknowledging his absence was like opening the door to find a familiar oak in the yard felled by an overnight storm. That old border collie, whose story and whose name I never knew, is an important memory from our twenty-three years on that Austin street.

BUNNY

Scarlett Spivey

Another great source of story material is family. All of us have "characters" in our families, folks who seem to march to their own musical soundtrack which we cannot hear. Scarlett Spivey's grandmother was the inspiration for some probing questions about faith and the presence of God.

As a young child, I knew the life of my family was defined by our belief in Christ and our regular church attendance. We each had a role in the life of the church: my mom was a member of the choir, my dad served as a church deacon and superintendent of Sunday Schools, and my brother and I were members of Sunday School, Training Union and Sunbeams. In addition to family worship on Sunday morning, Sunday evening, and Wednesday evening, we also attended revivals tossed in once or twice a year.

Being raised with a Christian foundation made me feel I was a follower; however, it was not until age ten that I felt my own personal relationship with Christ take root and I felt ownership of it.

This realization took shape with the health of my maternal grandmother. For years, she was hospitalized with schizophrenia and confusion, and in my child's mind I felt I could help her by turning to God's son in prayer asking that she be healed.

Her name was Leona, but as a toddler I named her "Bunny." She had a heart-shaped face with high cheek bones, a beautiful smile, a perfectly shaped model's body, and had fine taste in nice clothing. My favorite photograph of her was taken on a downtown Dallas street corner during the 1940s, with her blonde hair styled in soft curls that peaked out of her stylish hat. Complimenting her hat was her smart linen suit outlined with piping in a contrasting shade.

I remember during one hospital visit with Bunny, she gave me a plastic ivory-colored ring with a crude, rustic carving of someone looking like Davy Crockett with a coon-skin cap. During our six-hour car trip home, my mom shared that she regularly prayed for her mother to be well and to be able to live independently. I decided right there in the car that I, too, could add my prayers; helping me remember would be the ring on my finger, the only material gift that I ever received from my grandmother.

For about a six-week period, I prayed every night before going to sleep. And the plastic ring was on my finger continuously. I wondered what was taking God so long to hear my prayers. I knew He could do anything; in Bible stories, numerous tales of healing-miracles recorded the power of Jesus as he instructed the lame to "rise up" and the blind to see.

Then, one day on the school playground the plastic ring broke. In my sadness and disappointment, I threw it away. However, my overpowering feeling was confusion with God for not healing Bunny. Why wasn't He listening to my nightly prayers?

That night I did not pray. And it was months before I resumed my ritual of talking with God. I recall thinking, "God must not love me or Bunny." My emotions were raw and I needed time to heal and to mature. I continued my church attendance with my family, but the experience felt different for me. I had so many questions; did I do something wrong and that was God's reason for not answering my prayer? Was I too impatient? Was God's answer just about to come?

A lesson on patience would require time for me to sift through the facts I knew and the feelings I had. How was my grandmother able to keep any shred of her dignity during her lucid moments, while facing daily surroundings of cold metal bars, peeling paint, and virtually no privacy? I often wondered if her 24-hour experience was the same as my 24-hour experience. Perhaps God was there with her through the turbulent days which turned to weeks, then to months, eventually to years and finally to decades.

While I still search for answers, I do know that God granted Bunny a long life of 80 years. And although she never lived outside the hospital setting after age 40, I was able to visit her and eventually introduce my three children, her great-grandchildren, to her. By this time in my life, I knew God did love me and my grandmother.

Only time and patience helped me appreciate these true blessings.

AN UNPRECEDENTED OPPORTUNITY

Stan Lackey

All I can say is that whenever I read something Stan has written, I can be sure that it's going to be unlike anything else I've ever read. That's not a small thing; a unique style and vision are things every writer should strive for. I'm so glad we have Stan in our group…but federal law prohibits more than one Stan Lackey per zip code. Every time I read this little tale, it makes me laugh all over again.

The best advice I ever got was from my father. He told me along with my other brothers and sisters that we should expect once in our life—but maybe not more than once—an unprecedented opportunity. He said it could come in a variety of forms, but when it did—seize it! He also said to not let it get away because it won't be back your way again; you can count on that. He told me privately that I might not get one to the same degree as my siblings, so I needed to keep an extra keen eye out for mine. I did, but many years passed before it arrived.

It began on my twenty-first birthday, January 13, 1973. With few friends and practically no chance of a surprise party coming my way, I decided to celebrate the event by going horseback riding. When you live in Tuckahoe, Virginia there's no shortage of riding ranches, and I found one just north of town in Hanover County, the Hidden Hills Riding Stables.

After assessing my riding skills and experience, they determined that I should ride with a group of ten-year-olds who were also celebrating a birthday. So, I ended up going to a birthday party any-way! It was quite festive with balloons tied around the horses' necks, and the kids were all so excited that they didn't mind that I was going to tag along.

My horse was called Buck-O. He was given that name because at one time he was rather high spirited, but he had grown out of that phase and proved to be a wonderful and gentle companion for our two-hour ride. He wasn't constantly stopping to eat grass or trying to turn around and head back to the barn. Buck-O seemed to take professional pride in providing me a pleasant, non-combative ride. He was a little on the small side, had one milky eye that he couldn't see out of, and his color was best described as mottled, but he responded with a gleeful snort when petted or talked to.

After the ride, I found the owner of the ranch and asked how much it would take to buy Buck-O. The owner said that Buck-O was getting close to becoming dog food and would bring in twenty-five cents a pound, but if I could come up with the same amount he'd board him for an extra thirty a month. That next week I gave him $290, that got me Buck-O and three months of boarding. I was now a horseman, and only four months away from my once-in-a-lifetime opportunity.

It came on May 21, 1973. I was riding—Buck-O was mostly walking—down the back roads of the Virginia hill country. We came to a beautiful ranch entrance with the name Meadow Farm over the archway. People are friendly to strangers in Virginia even now, but back then especially, and especially to horse people—of which I was one.

I led Buck-O toward the barn, but as I got closer I could see horses, a lot of activity, and a lot of activity around one giant of a red horse. The whole place was like some kind of first rate equine center with its very own race track. Before I could get too close, a young Mexican man ran over asking us what we were doing there. I told him I wanted some water for my horse (I loved hearing those words come out of my mouth), but he just pointed at the big red horse and said, "Do you know who that is?" I had heard people use that exact phrase before but never about a horse. I told him that I had no idea who that was. He put his hands on his hips, cocked his head and said, "Secretariat…that's who." Then he just looked at me. The look said, "So, why don't you and this cootie with a saddle on it go back to the leper colony you rode in from, because the road apples from that horse over there are worth more than you and your nag put together."

I was less concerned about the look and more about what he had said, "Secretariat!" The horse that had just won the Kentucky Derby three weeks ago, then won the Preakness last week, and would be going for the Triple Crown at Belmont Park in two weeks. I instinctively asked, "Can I ride him?" The young man replaced the "I" in that sentence with a "you" and screamed it back at me—over and over and louder and louder. I quickly knew that my request was out of the realm of possibility, but I also knew this was it. That moment my father had told me about, and Buck-O and I were going to seize it!

The screaming got the attention of an older man with silver hair. He turned out to be Lucien Laurin, Secretariat's trainer. He asked what was going on, and before the other guy could answer I did. "Buck-O and I want to race Secretariat."

This got me another stare. Finally, the trainer flipped a thumb at my horse and asked, "This is

Buck-O?" I assured him it was, and he assured me that Secretariat was preparing for the Belmont, and he had no intention of racing a carnival pony. I asked if he was going to race Secretariat around that track over there, and, if he was, I didn't see why I couldn't race with him. He did, and he turned and walked off. My once-in-a-lifetime was slipping away.

I had to do something, so I yelled out, "If Buck-O beats Secretariat, I'll swap you horses straight-up!" I didn't want to give-up Buck-O, of course, but if he could beat Secretariat he deserved to have the best facilities and trainers possible. The man stopped dead in his tracks. His back was still to me, but I could see he was starting to tremble. Good! I had gotten him mad enough to race me! But to my surprise, he started laughing so hard that I thought he was going into a seizure. It went on for a good minute and everybody came over to see what was so funny. Mr. Laurin had his hands on his knees and was laugh-crying as he tried to explain to the men. "Swap…Secretariat…for…Buck-O!!"

The men finally figured it out, and soon everyone was laughing—except me. I'd had about enough and yelled, "I mean it. If my horse wins, you can take Buck-O to the Belmont!"

This, too, did not have the effect I had hoped. Mr. Laurin literally fell onto his rear-end laughing. He kept repeating, "Take…Buck-O…to…the Belmont!" I waited as patiently as I could, nearly two more minutes, before Mr. Laurin finally was able to speak. Sitting in the dirt and drying his eyes, he said, "Son, I haven't laughed that good since…this whole Triple Crown thing got…oh, boy. Sure, you can race Big Red. I owe you that. Bring your…Buck-O on over." He started laughing again as I walked Buck-O over to the track.

I took him to the starting line and mounted-up. One of the groomsmen asked if Buck-O wanted blinders. I said he'd just need one, but he told me they only came in pairs, so I said no. When they brought Secretariat over, I noticed two things: he was huge and he didn't like Buck-O; and he kept trying to nip him. Good ol' Buck-O just took it in stride. Even Secretariat was taking notice of my horse!

The training track at Meadow Farm is a half-mile oval. Mr. Laurin said he wanted Secretariat to go one and an eighth mile—a little more than two times around. When the race started I honestly thought we were going to win, but that was only because Secretariat had initially refused to run. It was like Buck-O had befouled his track. I started to look back again, but Secretariat was now rushing by me so quickly I almost fell off Buck-O. As he went by, Secretariat tried to nip his ears again, but he was going too fast—Secretariat, that is.

We, of course, got one more fly-by from Secretariat, and he ended up beating us by over a quarter of a mile. Matter of fact, by the time we finished, Secretariat was already in his stall getting brushed-down. Mr. Laurin was very nice, and gave Buck-O some oats and water. When we shook hands goodbye, he said Buck-O was a fine horse. I looked him in the eyes and said smiling, "You don't have to tell me!"

All the way back to the riding ranch I kept telling Buck-O how proud I was of him, and that finishing second to Secretariat was no shame. But mostly I thanked him for giving me my once-in-a-lifetime event. Even after Buck-O was struck by lightning and died that next month, I got to tell everybody I met—sometimes just strangers on the street—about the day I raced Secretariat. At his grave the marker says: Buck-O, he lost to Secretariat, but beat him to Heaven. The book of Revelation says that when the Lord returns he'll be riding a horse…I won't be surprised if it's Buck-O.

So, you can imagine my surprise when the very next year I got another once-in-a-lifetime! I had taken a job delivering product for a medical supply company in Pennsylvania. One day they gave me a box of bandages, anti-inflammatory medicine, stitching supplies, and some other pretty routine stuff to take up to Deer Lake, Pennsylvania. As I drove through the woods, I kept wondering what could possibly be out here in the middle of nowhere…a logging company?

Obviously, when I came to the end of the road and saw a boxing ring I was a bit confused. A large black man asked what I wanted, and I told him I had an order for a Dr. Pacheco. Dr. Pacheco was very pleasant, and he explained that this was the training camp for Muhammad Ali. Wow! I told Dr. Pacheco that I was a huge fan of the Champ's, and I just knew he was going to beat George Forman next month in Africa.

Dr. Ferdie—as they all called him—asked if I wanted to see Ali's afternoon sparring session. He didn't have to ask twice.

As we walked to the ring, I was getting that same funny feeling I had had the day I met Secretariat—that this could be another moment of unprecedented opportunity. I could almost hear my father say, "Seize it."

I was mesmerized seeing the Champ in the ring. He looked even bigger and more handsome in person. But something was wrong. Several people were talking to him, and he didn't seem pleased. Dr. Ferdie told me to wait there and he joined the discussion in the ring.

A few moments later, he explained that there wouldn't be an afternoon session. It seemed that one sparring partner had left that morning for a family emergency, and the other had hurt his shoulder in the morning session.

This was no coincidence; the Hebrews don't even have that word in their vocabulary. No, this was my David and Goliath moment, and I seized it! I said, loud enough for Ali to hear, "I'll fight you, Champ."

Everyone stopped talking and looked over and down at me. Ali took his mouthpiece out, frowned and said, "Boy, you ugly enough as it is. You get any uglier, and even yo' mama won't love you."

He didn't say it mean-spiritedly; he was just being Muhammad Ali. As everyone laughed it became clear that they weren't taking me seriously, and I needed to change that opinion quickly because the Champ was leaving the ring.

I hated to say what came out of my mouth next, but it was necessary. "Let's see, you paid Liston to take a dive, you didn't fight for your country, and now you won't fight me. Are you sure you really are a fighter?"

Ali froze, still bent under the ropes. He slowly stepped back into the ring and said, "Put some gloves on that fool." Bingo! They made me sign a waiver, gave me some gloves and a mouthpiece, and then somebody said "ding."

As I was coming to, about twenty-five minutes later, Dr. Ferdi said I lasted eight seconds in there with Muhammad Ali, but the really good news was that my jaw was not broken, only slightly dislocated. He put some ice on it, and told me to go straight to the hospital. I did, but not before I left Ali a card thanking him for the opportunity; that I hadn't meant what I had said, and that I wished him well in Africa next month. Two weeks later, about the time I was able to chew again, I received a boxing glove in the mail—the glove that had hit me—signed by the Champ.

For over thirty-five years my biggest problem was deciding which story I would tell strangers first; the day I raced Secretariat, or the day I boxed Muhammad Ali. I certainly never thought I would have another event that could even be comparable, let alone even greater than those two wonderful moments...until tonight.

Earlier today while I was crossing a ranch—Jim Preston said I could come onto his land as a short cut to the lake—I stepped into a bear trap that he had laid, probably to catch the wolf that was killing his stock. Well, I've got some bad news for Rancher Jim; he doesn't just have one wolf, he has a whole pack of them, and they're circling me right now. When my foot got caught in the bear trap I tried and tried to open it, but it would have taken two men, at least. I started screaming for help, and that—or the scent of my blood—probably attracted the wolves.

Fortunately, I had some paper and a pen in my backpack and wrote down everything you've just read and will read. On another piece of paper I've drawn a line down the middle and hope to complete the lists before they attack.

On the left side I've written the negative things about my current situation. That list includes: I'm stuck in a bear trap; I'm surrounded by twelve to fifteen hungry wolves; it's dark and I can't see too good; they can.

The list on the right side includes: since the wolves showed up, it's taken me out of my little pity-party over the fact that I'll probably lose that foot; I finished second in my two other once-in-a-lifetime events, so I'm due; getting attacked by wolves is even a better story than the Ali or Secretariat stories; it's a beautiful night; I've got my Boy Scout knife and, more importantly, another unprecedented opportunity.

THE WINDMILL

Darwyn Hanna

Darwyn finds beauty and meaning everywhere, not least in an old windmill which performs its assigned task for years, drawing little thought from most. But beauty—and poetry—are there for the taking.

A landmark of life
In my Dad's early prime
Has slipped to the rank
Of a landmark of time.

Magnifying the fury
Of a turbulent whipping gale
Fan racing to nowhere
With a zigzagging tail.

Glancing at the moving clouds
Straight up from the base
The windmill is falling
An illusion of their race.

Cypress tank a-standin' by
Seepin''tween the cracks
A heavy load for four stout posts
You'd think it'd break their backs.

A towering signal to quench a thirst
And stretch a travelers limbs
Or to wet rickety wagon wheels
Just to tighten up the rims.

A norther blowing has the the tank overflowing
And rain makes the field a lake
It protests with a moan, a screech and a howl
The setting of the brake.

On a summer day when the creek is dry
And the clouds are much too fickle
It's pulling at a deeper stream
For a pulsing little trickle.

Becalmed it looks fragile
While standing at ease
Peering over the land
For its muscle — a breeze.

The need of its fruit
Has now come full cycle
To harness the wind
For necessity and trifle.

White sentinels of power
That decorate our ridges
Filling an energy gap
That once had no bridges.

The slow moving blades
A metronome to slow our pace
The wind reflects life
Continuous but not a race.

ONLY BELIEVE

Patty Buchanan

If I had to sum up my 'ministry' in a few words, I would say it's been a search to find God in the smallest, most obscure and unlikely places. When you start looking for Him—outside the dusty black covers of your Bible—you'll be amazed where He shows up. Patty Buchanan knows exactly what I'm talking about.

The holidays can be difficult. For some of us, things are not what they should be...if measured by the merry TV ads and nostalgic songs on the radio. It's a bit like arriving at an airport, which can be a lively event greeted by joyful screams and happy chatter, but can also be an unfriendly feeling of emptiness, accompanied only by the whirring of a roller bag and the impersonal voice of security announcements in the background. Such was my arrival at 10:00pm on New Year's Eve 2009.

As my little green suitcase and I sat waiting for the shuttle, I pondered the fact that I was unemployed during a recession in a town where I knew few people. In an effort to be cheerful, I began a conversation with the girl sitting beside me. The trivial discussion about the bad weather and airport connections was suddenly interrupted by a bent, elderly shuttle driver, who smiled and asked us to come with him. Our number increased by two more people, who appeared to be married though they never spoke. We filed dutifully in the van and rumbled into the night, settling into the kind of silence where a cough seems out of place and the quiet takes on a presence no one wants to challenge. Not even coming to a halt behind the revolving red-blue-white lights of police cars and people sorting out an accident elicited a comment within the van. I considered starting a conversation more than once, but decided...why bother?

When the other travelers were methodically delivered to their destinations, I was alone with the driver. Assuming that his silence was out of duty, I was the first to speak, asking him whether I was his last fare and if he would go home soon. I was hoping that someone his age wouldn't have to work too hard.

"I'll be driving until 2:00 am," he said. He explained that he had been a postman, walking all over the city for thirty years delivering mail, and now he was driving all over the city delivering people. He seemed quite content with his 12 hour-per-day job, when a younger driver would probably be trying to figure out a way to do something besides working long hours on holidays—dealing with passengers anxious to get where they're going, angry if they're late, aggressive if they don't get their way, or sometimes just sad and solemn.

After we talked about his job, he inquired about mine. I replied that I was currently without one.

"God has protected me all my life and He will protect you too!" he announced and filled the van with colorful anecdotes. He was a happy man. As we bounced through the darkness, lit only by occasional street lamps casting yellow ovals on deserted streets, we talked about God's goodness and provision.

I decided that, although a tip was not required, I would give this kind little driver a two-dollar tip since it felt like the right thing to do (I had been counting every penny I spent for three months.). However, when I looked in my wallet, I discovered that I had one twenty-dollar bill and one five-dollar bill. I dug deep into both front pockets of my slacks, where I sometimes put a single bill or some coins, but nothing was there. I counted the change in my wallet, but decided that giving him a handful of coins might be insulting. Oh well, maybe he doesn't really need a tip anyway, I rationalized.

But something had shifted in my heart that had nothing to do with money. I knew that, whether or not it was warranted, I was going to give him the five-dollar bill. So I stuffed it into my right front pocket (convenient to retrieve while grasping my luggage later). We drove further into the outskirts of the city and the distant twinkling lights, as I reflected on how good it felt to be driven by someone who knew exactly where they were going. It had been a while since I had felt that way.

I was half wishing I could stay right there in that van with that feeling, as our conversation eased down to a predictable ending, and we pulled slowly through the apartment gate. He helped me out, set my luggage beside me and began to turn away.

"Wait! I want to give you five dollars." As soon as the words were out of my mouth, I thought, "Odd that I would have said it that way."

He started to chuckle as I slipped my hand into my right front pocket. But nothing was there. I dug into both pockets two more times. Nothing.

"Strange," I said out loud. "I was sure I put it there."

Confused, I reached again into my pocket. Out came a bill…a one dollar bill. Thinking that the five-dollar bill was probably there as well, I reached in again and pulled out another one dollar bill.

I heard him chuckle louder, as I pulled out three more…for a total of five dollars.

"Strange," I said again, knowing that I couldn't possibly have missed all five one-dollar bills.

As I handed him the money he smiled, told me to get some rest and trust that God would bring me a job. I told him to have a blessed New Year, although I sensed that he would anyway, with or without my blessing.

Still pondering the shell-and-pea game that God seemed to have played on me, I dragged my suitcase slowly up the stairs and into my silent apartment. The image of the lively little driver still haunted me; I wished I had asked for his name. I couldn't shake the feeling that something extraordinary had happened. For no particular reason, I reached into my right front pocket and felt something. I pulled it out.

It was the original five dollar bill.

Today, that five-dollar bill hangs prominently on my refrigerator door, held in place by a tattered rainbow magnet. Needless to say, I will never spend it. It reminds me that God always gives us what we need when we need it, and that His presence is as mysterious as it is constant.

FORGIVE, NOT FORGET
(AN EXCERPT FROM "BLOOD ON THE BED")

Karin Richmond

In 1983, Karin Richmond was the victim of a brutal attack in an historic Austin hotel, slashed and stabbed repeatedly by a hotel employee. She is currently finishing a book on her horrifying ordeal, her road back to health, and her work to help pass new legislation to protect others from such an "inside job" attack. It's a harrowing tale and Karin has chosen to write it in a unique fashion, telling not only her own story, but imagining the side stories of her attacker and some of the other people involved in the case. It's a bold tactic and a fascinating way to recount a truly amazing story. The following incident did occur at a bar in Austin about 15 years after Karin's assault. Some of the characterizations are fictionalized and the names are changed.

Over the years, I had pushed back, struggled and shoved into dark recesses the prospect of forgiving the angry man who became my enemy. For many years, no great strides were ventured, nor gained. But one night, an unexpected opportunity for forgiveness sat right down beside me, literally.

Henry Gonzales was getting ready for an informal "meet-'n'-greet" with a possible new employer. He was actually a friend of his from way back. So they chose a local bar near the capital complex.

Henry slipped into his Dockers, loosened his belt a notch and grabbed his dark brown jacket. He was getting older and disliked that his midsection had gotten wider over the years. But he was still fit overall and had plenty of experience and training in his field. And he still looked good. Henry kissed his wife as he strode out the door, giving her a little wink. He still loved her after all these years. She had given him a good family and reared his four children, now all out on their own (he gave himself a little sign of the cross . . . *In nomine Patris* . . .). And he had stood by her throughout her bout with breast cancer. Thank the Lord that he had been employed with a hotel back then with great health insurance benefits. Thank the Lord that she survived and was fully recovered (another sign of the Lord's cross).

It was about 5:00, early even for happy hour, but he wanted to scope out a good seat with a surrounding view. He always wanted to know who was coming in a place and kept his back to a wall if at all possible. In his line of work, anything could change on a dime and some habits just die hard.

He sat in the end chair of the bar and ordered a beer. Tall, in a frosted glass. He had a moment to himself, so a little reflection settled in. His prospects were good. He was on the shy side of middle age and kept up his marksman skills on a weekly basis. He was still employed, but the company he worked for was downsizing in this rotten economy and his department felt the pain. It was generous that he had been given a 60-day notice.

Catching a glint in the changing light of the glass entrance door, he looked up to see a woman entering the bar.

I swept into the room with an air of confidence and familiarity. I was an accomplished lobbyist and could not begin to remember all the stories that unfolded here. It was a legislative hot spot and during session, I could easily meet an elected official. Meet and drink with, that is. My companion was not yet to be seen, and in fact the place was pretty empty—I checked my watch again—and it was still on the early side of happy hour. But there was a guy sitting at the bar. A quick up-and-down look told me he might be good company while waiting just a bit. "This seat taken?"

He was a little caught off-guard, but managed a quick grin. "Well, young lady, I am waiting on a fellow to join me but until then, the seat is all yours."

"That makes two of us" I returned the smile. "Hi, my name is Karin." He returned my firm handshake and gave me his full attention.

"Henry Gonzales."

He was formal, but quick on my comeback, I asked, "Henry or Enrique?". Henry is a gringo substitute for Enrique, but since I was familiar with this, I was polite to ask.

"No, not me, but it was my father's name."

We politely bantered back and forth, but the conversation slowed down when Henry shared with me that he was in the security business, mostly with large projects as a team leader. He had once been in the hotel security business, but had moved on from that line of work some time back.

I looked into his eyes, hard. "Were you here, in Austin, in 1983?".

"Yes, m'am, I have been here some 25 years now."

I glanced at the front door and around the bar to make sure my companion had not slipped in. All clear. I decided—rather impulsively—to share my story. Using a hushed tone and leaning toward him, I unwound the story of my brutal attack. Where it was, the year, the employee having a list of single women in a room, and him "wanting to kill a white woman." Henry's eyes grew wider at each turn of the story. His attention was rapt. I noticed that his body language was very still, too still. Something was off.

"It was me…I was in charge of security that night at the hotel."

I gasped. "What?!"

"I was supposed to be there that night. I had gone through all the check points, made sure all of the security equipment was on line and working—which it was. I rarely asked for a night off, but my wife was in the hospital. She had cancer then and I wanted to be with her. I spoke with my deputy guard and he was fine taking over, and the night manager said no problem with me going. I left about eight p.m. I got the call from my deputy about midnight. He had just left your room. He was nearly hysterical. After he calmed down, he told me what he saw and that he had called the police and an emergency vehicle. The weird thing was that the bartender was already there and there was this other hotel guest in his boxer shorts!"

He paused to collect himself. He was visibly upset.

"He told me it was one of our guys that did this to our guest. It was the new Sampson guy with Maintenance. 'How do you know?' I asked him, already wary of a lawsuit. 'She is still alive, she is really beat up, but she is still conscious and is talking. The guest identified her assailant as our guy—he still has on his uniform and name badge.' "

"By the time I got back to the hotel, Karin, you were gone. The emergency team had you to the hospital fast. I was there getting the story of the situation down and talking with our bartender and the police when a call came over the radio to let the police look in the room again. We had already locked the door as a crime scene."

"I don't know how, but someone tipped off the police to go back to the room and search for the weapon, a knife. I let the officers in and this time they were on their hands and knees looking for a knife. They had to be careful not to get in all the blood and glass. One of them popped a flashlight under the bed skirt under the bed. 'Found it!' and showed the knife to me. It was not a hotel knife and I told the police that. It must have been a personal weapon."

Henry leaned forward to her. "Karin, I never knew what happened to you after that night. The hospital would not release any information about you. Until this moment, I did not know if you lived or died from that attack…the attack that happened on my watch!" The man's shoulders began to sag. His eyes were moist. "Karin, this is the nightmare that any of us in the hotel security business dread. This is the fear each of us live with. This is the event we are supposed to protect our guests from and I failed at the task. Over all these years, I have asked myself over and over, had I been there and not taken off to see my wife, would this have happened?

"You know, after a few years I had to quit the security business for hotels. I just could not bear the idea that something like that would ever happen to an innocent guest.

"Would you forgive me?"

I softly enclosed my hands over his. He saw the scars that remained on my hand from my defensive wounds. His eyes misted over. I quietly replied, "Henry, it is all right. It is Okay. See these? See how they have healed? I have healed, too. I am physically okay. There is no need for you to carry this burden with you any longer. It was not your fault…and I do forgive you. I forgive you with all that I am and still hope to be." Both of our eyes met for one more deep encounter. Henry managed a small fleeting smile before the glass door opened and my companion strode inside the bar.

Sissy! YAY! The first of many I hope! Love Marty
P.S. We need to go gather some more material! Ciao! ☺

VENICE IN THE "HOOD"

Marty McAllister

It's been exciting and gratifying to see the variety of genres in which our SCRIBE writers work. I knew we would have poets and short story writers and memoirists…but I confess I did not expect to receive a travel essay, though every bookstore has a substantial shelf of travel writing. Marty McAllister is an accomplished traveler and her detailed depiction of a single day in Venice will make you want to pack your bags and dust off your passport.

Outside my shuttered windows it is a lonely quiet, early morning before dawn; just occasional footsteps on the campo or nearby bridges that cross the small canals. No sounds of commerce. Birds sound as if they are screaming. There are no insects; I saw one fly in five days. No cars.

About 6:00am, I hear the sound of a few small boats starting their engines. In other areas, grocery boats, garbage, ambulance, police boats, and public transportation boats called *vaporetti* are doing the same. Locals and tourists alike must walk or take boats to begin their day's activities.

I unfasten the small metal latches, push open the green wooden shutters and fold them back to see the unadorned façade of chiesa San Martino watching over my tiny second floor apartment. A footbridge over a narrow canal separates me from the campo that is home to the church and *negozio di alimentari*, a grocery store. I can see the yellow seven-story building where my landlords live on the third floor and run the grocery store at street level. Smaller than a one-car garage, it stocks a variety of staples, cheeses, deli meats, olives, dairy products, water, juice, pastas and wines.

Close to 7:00am the sounds begin: clanging, banging, opening, shutting, motors and voices. At the grocery, metal security gates roll up, followed by the spreading of large, green awnings. I hear a few footsteps, then more on the two metal bridges connecting the walkways on either side of my flat.

Deliverymen, sounds of commerce, locals walking to work or tourists up early due to jet lag. All are part of my morning wake-up call.

Francesco steps out of his grocery store to meet a man rolling a small red plastic crate attached to a dolly. The deliveryman stops in front and together they carry small packages into the store. Cheese delivery? A few well-rounded older women stroll by. Tourists or locals? I decide by their casual, unhurried demeanor, lack of luggage or cameras, and mode of dress, that they are locals. The putt-putt of boat engines and workers pushing and pulling containers up and down the steps of nearby bridges continue through mid-morning.

Venetians refer to the city as "*Serenissima*" meaning "most serene." The ancient and modern mix in a frenzy of shopkeepers, restaurateurs soliciting passers-by, street artists, sellers of kitschy souvenirs, and tour guides holding up their closed umbrellas to herd their charges through the day-trip visits. Those who return to the mainland at night miss the magical evenings in exchange for a less expensive hotel.

Sometimes called the most beautiful city built by man, and Europe's most romantic city, Venice has another side. The ancient façades have been witness to more than 1000 years of luxurious lifestyles, ruthless rule of powerful religious leaders, extensive commerce and trade as a major maritime power and the lives of countless writers, artists and musicians. History is present and alive in this city of huge palaces and churches built on sticks planted into the mud of the lagoon over a thousand years ago.

I rented an apartment in the sestiere Castello, one of six neighborhoods, in an area where Venetians live and work. Just outside the tourist mainstream are quaint places with locals who are willing to offer glimpses into authentic Venetian lifestyle. This is where I spend most of my time.

Only a short walk from the lagoon, I find my way to the apartment easily now. The first time I stayed, it took me more than a week to discover the shortcut leading me to the familiar location next to a hotel I knew.

Behind the hotel, a walkway winds into several turns on unmarked paved paths between buildings. Around a corner, down a narrow walk and over two bridges brings me to the large green door where I use the first of two keys. Once inside, I walk up the stairway and use the second key. The one-room apartment has three large shuttered windows. I would grow to love the glimpses of life they would offer of the Campo San Martino and the narrow canals that run alongside the buildings. Large wooden beams stripe the ceiling above a double bed, a small kitchen area, and a table with four chairs set in the corner between two of the windows. The bathroom is just behind the kitchen with shower and bidet, along with sink and toilet. A built-in closet along one wall and some antique furniture complete the comfortable apartment.

Due to fear of being lost, during my first stay I used the well-traveled route to the lagoon, finding it infallible. My wariness was partly due to observation. From my window, I had witnessed several frustrated tourists studying their maps, irritated with each other for getting lost and wondering how to get back to familiar territory. From my window I would politely ask, in English, "May I show you how to get back to Piazza San Marco?"

Startled, they would look up and nod.

"Okay. I'll be right down."

Occasionally I was stopped as I walked and asked in halting Italian, "*Dove' il …?*" (Where is…?)

I would answer, "Do you want me to tell you in Italian or English?"

Invariably, the response would be, "English," except for one time when the women were French, in which case I answered them in French to the best of my travel-talk recall.

Tourists don't know this hidden enclave and can't find it, or at least can't find their way out, so they seldom venture there. I found it because I attended a language school that assigned me a living arrangement for two weeks. I have returned many times.

After a restful morning, I venture out to buy groceries. At the nearby *alimentari*, I buy fruit juice in a box, wine, water, taleggio, pecorino, and gorgonzola cheeses, along with fresh olives in a piquant oil mix. For bread I wander down the narrow walkway to the *pane negozio* and for produce to the *frutta e verdure*. Tourists who are not aware of the *de rigueur* at the fruit and vegetable stands are quickly admonished if they try to select produce by actually picking it up. The customer points as the shopkeeper places selected items in a paper sack, weighs them and then accepts payment. The tiny shops are sometimes crowded but one must simply wait in turn for service. Rushing is not in the vocabulary.

After delivering my groceries, I venture off to revisit some of my favorite areas of Venice. On my way to the lagoon, I stop at a neighborhood café for a quick espresso, three euros cheaper here than in Piazza San Marco. I stand at the counter to drink rather than sit outside at a table because sitting is more expensive. I politely greet the server in Italian, using basic words that every tourist should attempt to learn.

"*Buongiorno signore. Come sta oggi?*"

"*Bene grazie.*"

"*Ciao. Buona giornata.*"

Hi, how are you? Fine thanks. Bye. Have a good day.

Along the lagoon I see Chiesa San Giorgio, set on its own island. Its campanile (bell tower) offers a spectacular view of the entire area, especially of Piazza San Marco, the campanile, Palazzo Ducale and the Basilica. It's a quick *vaporetto* trip and memorable view.

Napoleon described Piazza San Marco as "the finest drawing room in Europe." All other open spaces in Venice are referred to as campos or piazzettas; only San Marco is a piazza. The enormous trapezoidal space is enclosed on three sides with a several-storied arched colonnade. Shops, restaurants and cafes line the covered walkway, tempting tourists as they pass. Several famous cafes space themselves along the gallery walk, with tables and chairs arranged to feature a small stage for the musicians. The Café Quadri opened in 1775 and sits across the piazza from the Caffè Florian, which opened in 1720. Small musical ensembles entertain passers-by as well as those seated at tables arranged near the stage of each café. At times, the musicians cooperate and take turns playing selections. Other times it is more like a battle of the bands.

My personal favorite is Caffè Florian, named after the first owner, Floriano Francesconi. The Florian has a rich history of well-known writers, artists, philosophers, and musicians as regular patrons. Goethe, Goldini, Byron and Casanova are just a few. Here I met a self-announced descendant of Casanova, who was attempting to prove his bloodline, rather unsuccessfully, although he was marginally entertaining.

The public boats called *vaporetti* are readily available but if time permits, I prefer walking. It is easy and fun to get lost in Venice but helpful signage does exist, to a limited extent. On the corners of some buildings, above the large shop windows there are yellow signs with relevant locations, along with an arrow pointing the way. San Marco, Academia, and Rialto are the main directional indications. Maps are only marginally helpful. I walk toward Academia, the only wooden bridge in Venice. After crossing over to sestiere Dosoduro, I wind my way toward Campo Santa Margherita and to my school.

On the way I stop at the "veggie boat." Always at the same footbridge, the long slender vessel sits, loaded with carefully stacked produce of every kind and color. One man sits on a stool near the boat, next to a barrel filled with water. He grabs an artichoke from a large pile, begins hacking away at the leaves and in less than a minute has the perfectly shaped heart ready to throw into the barrel where it floats among parsley leaves until purchased. Amazed at his speed, I watch for a few minutes before purchasing a few. As I have done in the past, I will boil these luscious artichoke hearts until tender, then toss them with the oil from the olives I bought at the negozio. The sliced garlic and spices in the oil, salt, pepper and a little balsamico vinegar combine to make the perfect taste, finished with a light broil.

Near my language school, I stop for a cappuccino, order at the counter inside and then sit outside as I did with my school friends during the pause between classes. On the first day, although I had not studied Italian formally, I was placed in the intermediate group. Obviously I didn't understand everything because, instead of taking the break, I thought class was over and left for the day. The next day, I understood. This neighborhood is another where few tourists venture. Everything is less expensive and the ordinary Venetians go about their ordinary day.

I wander back along the lagoon and stop into the Hotel Gabrielli for a favorite salad. I visit with

Santé, the headwaiter and friend, and order the *insalata di gamberetti* (arugula with shrimp in olive/lemon dressing).

In early evening I return to the Café Florian. Seated on one of the brown leather settees positioned against a gallery arch, I see clearly the discolored stone façade with top layer peeling and am captivated by its old world elegance. My half bottle of Da Vinci Chianti sits politely on the white marble top of the elaborately carved wooden table, along with a complimentary dish of cocktail nuts, olives and pretzels. I gaze at the decorative lettering above the door, gilding long since worn off, and at the aged mirrors and windows standing witness to times and visitors long gone.

As I have done many times, I ask Claudio, my waiter and friend who has worked here for over 30 years, if he can somehow get me a couple of the cherished etched Florian wine glasses. They are not for sale, and I want them instead of the others in the shop. He will try. On my laptop, I open a file to show him some photos from past visits. One of us standing in front of the Café Florian, another of me posing coquettishly in front of the stage with musicians playing, and others of the Romanian musical ensemble that I got to know.

Tourists crowd into the tiny café, both inside and along the covered gallery outside, while tables and chairs surrounding the canopied stage fill quickly. I move to a table on the Piazza facing the stage. The orchestra begins its first set of the evening and a shadow of melancholy creeps over me as I think of the musicians whose faces and names I knew well. The music varies but is mostly classical with a strong gypsy influence. At the break, I chat with the clarinet player and ask him to play my favorites, as the Romanians used to do. "Oblivion" by Piazzola and "Concerto di Araquez" by Rodrigo. As I listen, frozen in time, the blue sky blends gently to black in contrast with golden glow of the softly lit Basilica. The music continues. Claudio brings my check, cover charge for music deleted, along with a small Café Florian sack. In it I discover my coveted wine glass.

Further along the lagoon, I stop at the Hotel Danieli for a nightcap. Formerly a luxurious palazzo, the five-star hotel is not only elegant but has a stylish piano bar. I imagine myself as the *chatelaine* (lady of the castle) descending the red-carpeted staircase with grand arches backdrop, into what must have been the grand ballroom, moving gracefully through the elite invitees uttering the most charming of greetings.

This evening the performer is an extraordinarily handsome, 40-something man with curly hair, dark but greying distinguishingly, sensitive eyes and an enchanting voice. His mellow style blends perfectly with the ambience of the Grand Salone. My waiter suggested a chocolate martini that was *perfetto*. I lingered for one more, sketching patterns from the walls, windows and delicately carved bench nearby. Columns, painted ceiling, marble floors, tapestried walls and enormous glass chandeliers combine in perfection. A magical evening alone. I didn't need anyone or anything else. Elegant surroundings, beautiful music and my notebook complete me. Oh, and a beverage or two.

Seems so simple really.

Back in my apartment, voices and footsteps echo against the tightly nested buildings. The sounds of night come with mystery and slight surprise. A motorboat turns the corner in the canal below my window. Partygoers are celebrating riotously as their boat continues into the neighboring canal. I am relieved their destination is somewhere else. Several people walk past as the boat disappears. Their steps echo and their voices sound louder than necessary. Innate ambience notwithstanding, there is little regard for personal quiet here in the "hood."

Small groups and couples happen by late at night. Occasionally someone is pulling a heavy suitcase across a bridge, clunking loudly with each up and down step. Stereos and televisions can be heard, along with a rattling of dishes at mealtime. Sounds travel sharply through open windows and crack into otherwise silence. The same sounds that made me lonely on the first night are now part of my routine. Comfortable and like home. They are now my sounds.

GOD'S LOVE LANGUAGE

Lee Ann Penick

Only a few years ago, none of us knew the word "blog" or what it meant. Short for "web log," blogs have become the first sort of publication available to virtually any writer. At little or no cost, you can set up your own site where you can share your daily/weekly/monthly diary entries, rants, anecdotes or—as Lee Ann Penick has discovered—your devotional thoughts. This is a sample from her blog, which you can find at <u>lapenick.wordpress.com</u>*.*

I am still regaining my footing after reading *90 Minutes in Heaven* by Don Piper. For those of you who have read my initial reflection on this book, you'll recall that the word "praise" or the phrase "praise God" became speed bumps in my reading. I am regularly slowed down during my Bible readings when I come upon the phrase, "praise God." I read the book two months ago, and I am *still* awed by the importance of praising God.

In the book *The 5 Love Languages*, author Gary Chapman articulates the five main ways we express love to another individual: 1) Words of Affirmation, 2) Quality Time, 3) Receiving Gifts, 4) Acts of Service, and 5) Physical Touch. Most of us can read this list and know without much thought which one is the most meaningful to us. I enjoy spending quality time with those I love, as well as receiving gifts, receiving help from others on an unsolicited basis, and hugs. Those are all very nice and certainly not to be discounted, but the love language I find most powerful is words of affirmation.

I have come to believe that praise is God's love language. We can spend quality time with Him, do acts of service in His name, give a smile or a hug to someone who just needs one, and give gifts to others just to bless them with the love of Christ. God sees everything that we are doing and saying in His name and is pleased by those expressions of His love. But when you get right down to it, we can't touch God, and there is nothing we can offer others without His power and His resources. So what does that leave us that we can truly give Him? I think the answer is our heart, expressed through affirmations, or praise. I think He feels deeply loved by us when we just spend time expressing our love, letting Him know how much we really adore Him.

Acts 17:24-25 says, "The God who made the world and everything in it is the Lord of heaven and earth and does not live in temples built by hands. And he is not served by human hands, as if he needed anything, because He himself gives all men life and breath and everything else". (I invite you to re-read this verse and put your name in it. It becomes even more powerful.) Doesn't this passage say it all? He doesn't really "need" me or my services. So what is left is recognizing that we exist because He wants to enjoy us and for us to enjoy the personal love relationship He offers to each of us. The only thing I can really offer is what He really wants—praise, or words of affirmation. I want to love God the way He wants to be loved. I will be intentional to praise Him because that's what He desires.

I am made in His image. Is it any surprise that what He wants from me is the same thing I really want from others? These last two months of praising God intentionally has been a wonderful growing experience for me. Since I believe praise is God's love language, I am more intentional about praising God with words of affirmation, and I have found it to be a most enjoyable way of just connecting with Him.

Blessings,
Lee Ann

BLUE EYES

Dana Hood

When I announced the guidelines for submissions to this book, Dana told me that she couldn't even write a check in 2500 words. But sometimes, taking on a new genre or a new restriction opens creative doors we didn't know were there. Dana came up with this suspenseful story and she was even a couple hundred words under the limit.

As if her mood had spilled over into her cup, Cheryl found the dark void of the empty coffee mug disconcerting.

"What's your problem, Cher?" The perky blonde across the table leaned over and peered into the cup that had captured Cheryl's rapt attention.

"Ya need more coffee, hon? Geeze, allow me. " She got up, filled the cup and placed it before Cheryl who'd yet to look up.

"Thank you Gina. But coffee's not gonna make this go away."

"Well no, but you're acting like you've committed the crime of the century. All you did was turn the guy down. I'd imagine guys like him get turned down for dates all the time."

Cheryl looked up at her smiling friend and took a sip of the coffee. "I know. But maybe I should have said yes. He's sent me six texts today alone." She pushed the fall of dark curls away from her face. "He's not a bad guy, just a little over-eager, you know?"

"I guess. Do what you want, but I think he's a creeper. He's always standing there, just staring. And those eyes…they're so dark they're like zombie eyes." Gina quelled a mock shiver and laughed, "Lose it and move on, Cher."

As Gina was leaving, Cheryl looked up to see the object of her distraction enter the break room.

She smiled tentatively.

He flashed a movie star smile in her direction. "Hey, blue eyes."

"Hi James. How are you today?" She put on an artificial smile and pretended that she didn't feel like such a heel.

"Did you get my texts?"

"Oh. Yes, I was just reading them. I was getting ready to send you something."

"Uh-huh." James shook his head and smiled. "You were not."

"Ok. I wasn't." She dipped her head to hide her embarrassment. Slowly, she broached the subject that had been weighing on her mind. "You know, I feel kind of like a creep, shutting you down the way I did."

James seated himself at the table across from her. "You don't need to. You're not into me, that's cool." He sat back and a Cheshire cat grin curled his lips. "Don't know what you're missing, but hey, that's your loss." He was amused, but Cheryl's nervous laugh made him rethink his words. "Look, I was kidding. I'm not offended, really."

"Well, I was kind of mean…what if I treated you to dinner tonight?"

Her words came out in such a rush, he questioned her sincerity. So James merely quirked an eyebrow and chuckled. "Not necessary. I pretty much live in the friend zone with most women. Trust me, this is nothing new and I'm ok."

"Oh, great. Now I feel really bad. Please let me make you dinner. When was the last time you had a home-cooked meal?"

"Well, it's been a long time…"

"Then I'll see you at eight tonight." Cheryl wrote her address on a slip of paper and slid it across the table.

James smiled and took it and put it in his pocket. "Ok. Eight it is." He glanced at his watch and stood, "Speaking of time, I'm got a meeting. See you later, blue eyes."

As he left, Cheryl wondered if she was doing the right thing. James was a nice guy. Well-liked in the company, successful. Good-looking too, if you could get around the geeky haircut and the Clark Kent vibe he gave off. "Heck, I guess even Superman was kind of a nerd," she reasoned as she went back to her desk.

The work day wore on and on her way back from lunch, Cheryl got a text from James. It read, "**hey, blue eyes, looking forward to our time together tonight**." Cheryl found it odd, but was sweet. Very characteristic of what she knew of James thus far. Twenty minutes later she received another text.

"**you didn't answer me, blue eyes. Aren't you looking forward to our date?**"

Cheryl texted back, "Yes, I'm sorry but I'm really busy. I'll talk 2 U tonight."

The text reply, "**I hope this is the start of something**" came buzzing in moments later. Taken aback by the comment, she wondered again if she'd done the right thing but then shrugged it off as James being the perpetual eager beaver.

The afternoon was busy in her department; Cheryl rushed to make sure her presentation was complete before she settled in to getting the rest of her work wrapped up before the weekend. As she sat at the computer, her cell phone buzzed away on her desk.

"**hey blue eyes, do I need to bring anything tonight?**"

She replied, "No, just yourself."

"**that will be easy. almost as easy as looking at you.**"

She smiled and texted back, "Sweet, but you can't see me right now or you'd call off our date for sure! LOL!"

"**I can see you and you're beautiful. I like your hair up like that.**"

Cheryl swung around in her chair to face the glass walls of her office that looked out onto the sales floor. She'd expected to see James standing there making a face at her or something but no one was there.

"Where are you?" She hit the send button.

"**watching you.**"

She stood and went to the door of her office and peered out. Everyone was working at their desks or on the phone. No sign of James anywhere. Puzzled, she simply responded, "I don't see you."

"**no. you don't.**"

"Well, I'm going back to work – silly. C U later."

Just before five, Cheryl made a trip to the ladies room and on her way out, she ran into Gina.

"Hey, you got plans for tonight? Some of us are going to that new club a few blocks over." Gina waggled her eyebrows comically. "Hot men, lots of booze…"

Cheryl rolled her eyes. "Sounds like a blast. However, I have asked James over for dinner."

Gina slapped her hand to her forehead. "You are as softhearted as that big goof is. You should enjoy each other's company." Gina laughed and shook her head as she went into the restroom. "Have fun. If you get bored, you know where we are!"

Cheryl smiled as she went back her office to gather up her belongings. Her cell phone buzzed with another text from James. "**hey, I don't remember your address. Could you…?**"

She shook her head. Perhaps Gina's description of big goof was appropriate. She texted, "You lost it already? Tsk-tsk. Here it is…"

"thanks. so, see you at seven?"

"No. Eight! You need to write things down if you can't remember. I'm going to get a complex."

"I might forget the little things, but I can close my eyes and see every feature of your face, every curve of your body," came the reply.

Cheryl shook off the discomfort caused by the comment. She reasoned that James was apparently more socially awkward than she'd imagined. She turned to see him standing at the door of her office.

"Oh!" She clasped her hand to her chest. "You scared the hell out of me!"

Looking flustered, James stepped back out of the door way to make room for her to pass. "I am so sorry! I was just poking my head in before you left for the day."

She relaxed. "Oh well, of course. Are you headed out now too?"

"Soon. I've got some stuff to tie up first, but I'll be out of here shortly. Hey, is there anything I can bring tonight?"

Cheryl looked at him and shook her head. "You really should write things down. No. Like I said, just bring yourself."

Puzzled, James smiled at the comment and turned to walk Cheryl to the elevator. "Uh. Yeah, I do have a lot on my plate. I misplace a lot of things."

"I'll say." The elevator opened and Cheryl got on. "See you soon."

She caught a glimpse of James waving absently, lost in his thoughts as the elevator door closed.

On her way home, Cheryl fretted over the odd comments that she'd gotten from James that day. She found it strange how in person he didn't seem nearly as forward as he did when he was texting. But, she assumed that he was in the grip of the same phenomenon that caused people to be very obnoxious on blogs or in email, but then be relatively mild in person. Maybe James was just one of those people who needed to be hidden to say what he was thinking.

That didn't suit her at all. She liked the men in her life to be forthcoming and honest. Perhaps though, maybe James what just what he seemed. A really nice, intelligent but socially awkward man.

"I guess I'll find out which that is tonight." She mused as she pulled up to her home.

The evening light had given way to darkness, which came somewhat early this time of year. She frowned as she opened the car door and saw that the porch light wasn't on. She sighed heavily and assumed that once again the bulb was out. Ever since the man had installed the new fixture it seemed to literally eat light bulbs. She stood in the faint light of her car's cab light, looking for her house key when she heard something that made her turn around.

"Who's there?" She took a few steps forward towards the porch just as her cell phone buzzed.

The text message read, "**it's only me.**"

Cheryl turned and spoke loudly into the darkness, "Not funny, James."

Her phone buzzed again. "**oh, I'm not trying to be funny. Perhaps you'll find my activities later to be funny.**"

She gasped as the phone buzzed again. "**but I doubt it.**"

Cheryl turned back to her car only to see his large figure standing between her and the door. She screamed and started running towards the street where the street light cast a bright pool onto the pavement. She heard footsteps and loud breathing as he struck out after her. He was closing in on her and she tried to speed up only to realize that he'd caught hold of her jacket and was trying to jerk her down to the ground. Her mind quickly went through a myriad of scenarios, trying desperately to find the strategy that would save her life as her body made its endless journey to the ground.

And then he was on her. His fetid breath washed across her face, filling her nostrils with the repulsive stench of old coffee and cigarettes.

His hands were on her breasts, pulling her delicate silk blouse apart—the buttons flew as he dug his fingers into her tender flesh.

She screamed, but it ended in a rough slap across her face. Cheryl tasted blood mixed with the salt of her tears as she started to beg. He said nothing, but she felt the cold steel of a blade on her throat.

And then, as swiftly as he was on her, he was gone.

In the faint light, she could see that someone had pulled him off of her and was struggling with him in the yard. Cheryl ran to the neighbor's door and pounded on it. The man inside ran to assist. Within moments, her attacker was subdued and she could hear police sirens growing louder.

She slid down onto the sidewalk and leaned on the streetlamp. James came and sat down next to her on the curb.

"You alright?"

Cheryl stared at him. She stood and frantically looked around to see her neighbor sitting on her attacker in the yard and the squad cars pulling into her drive.

"James?"

"Yeah. I was just pulling up when I saw that guy attacking you."

Incredulous, Cheryl let her mouth gape. "You are the one who saved me?"

"I guess so. Of course, your neighbor tilted the scales in my direction too…"

"Then who was that?" She stood staring as the police handcuffed her assailant.

"I don't know. But he's got to work in our building."

Her gaze swung back around to James. "How do you know that?"

"Because after we got him we got him pinned down, and started searching him for more weapons, I found my cell phone in his pocket!"

"He had your phone?"

James sighed and rubbed his forehead. "Yeah. I lost it today before lunch sometime. But I misplace things all the time so I figured it would turn up. Who knew that this joker had stolen it?"

He thought for a minute. "You know what's weird? That he was here with my phone on the same night we had a date planned. Freaky."

Cheryl scrubbed her hands over her face. "Yeah. Freaky. Remind me to tell you just how freaky over dinner."

James shrugged. "Well, you can tell me over dinner at a restaurant. You don't need to cook after a night like this."

She nodded in agreement as they started walking back towards her home. James paused and pulled a phone out of his pocket. "Hey. I found your cell on the ground." He handed it to her.

Cheryl pushed it away. "No thanks. I think I'm going on a cell vacation for a little while."

THE KNIFE IS HIDDEN

Lauren Kinzie

I saw an Easter pageant once in which a guy jumped out in a red satin devil costume, with horns and a pitchfork, to tempt Jesus. I just laughed. If only evil was that easy to recognize! Implements of danger, though, come in many guises. Sometimes we don't recognize them until we feel the wound.

The knife is hidden—

under layers of cocktails, traditions and comfort food.

The knife is hidden—

in the "charming fixer-upper" with the astronomical mortgage.

The knife is hidden

In the safe neighborhood, wide streets, blue-ribbon school,

and bionic PTA.

The knife is hidden,

beneath the blaring big-screen TV

and the Ethan Allen bedroom suite.

It is hidden in plain sight,

scarcely noticeable, just slightly off—

like outdated wallpaper.

It's in the bones of a home

and takes a veteran realtor to distinguish its character.

But, the hero-child

is an expert emotional excavator,

she ferrets out tensions, glares and tears

and takes ownership…

saving the day,

making everyone's everything okay.

She's human Feng Shui—

keeping neighborhood questions away.

Juggling, deflecting, peacekeeping, and dancing furiously…

she erases herself away.

Everyone's happier that way.

Feelings are fearsome things,

especially when they are her own.

Safer to be alone

where no one needs saving

no one is blaming or playing

pin the tail on the martyr.

Alone and quiet, she's just a child with the blanket

torn off of her bed.

It keeps her warm and safe

while she sleeps and plays.

Tomorrow, is another day.

If need be, she will wear it as her cape instead.

HAVE YOURSELF A SCARY LITTLE CHRISTMAS

Lisa Robertson

Lisa Robertson grew up in Dripping Springs, Texas, where something very much like this incident may or may not have happened, depending on the statute of limitations.

There had to be a reason a 13-year-old was looking down the barrel of a shotgun. But at the moment, reason only seemed to be saying, "This gun can blow your head clean off!"

That was the moment I decided Christmas was the scariest holiday season.

I knew people were often sad at Christmas time. My mother made it her mission to invite non-relatives into our home for Christmas lunch. My questioning why always received the same answer. "People get depressed and lonely at Christmas," she would say. "They need to be with a family." Consequently, I also knew people were often tired at Christmas. Like my mother, who would launch into a cooking frenzy of the sort only equaled by a mess hall cook. And I also knew people who got really angry and grouchy at Christmas, like my mother got at my dad on Christmas night when he was reading the paper and she was cleaning up the mess. But I didn't know people got scared at Christmas.

A mature eighth-grader, I knew that for all the happy angels, the jingle bells, and the ho-ho-ho's, there was a side of Christmas that made adults act like it was Halloween. But in my mind Christmas was connected with birth. Not death. Especially not *my* death. I never thought the end would come as the words "figgy pudding" left my lips. "Figgy" and "dying" are words that should not go together.

But before my end, the beginning.

"Jeremiah was a bullfrog..." played on the turntable as I pulled on jeans, sneakers and several shirt layers so I'd be warm enough to make THE WALK tonight. It was THE major part of THE major

Christmas party.

Karen's Christmas caroling party, to be specific. The only teen party in our small town that wasn't a church- or school-sponsored event. It was basically a party where we would eat queso, chips and cookies and listen to music, then to close out the evening we would take THE WALK.

I made sure I got dropped off a little late. I didn't want to appear too eager. "Hey, Minton's here!" Great. Karen's little brother had to announce me. Though I have to admit, he was not so little any more. In fact that seemed to be happening to all the guys in my class. All of the sudden they seemed really tall and they all seemed to have laryngitis.

"Hey, Minton. Seen any good spit-wads lately? Ha ha." Charlie. Great just who I wanted to see, but before I could get off a snappy comeback I was surrounded by informants.

"Oh, my god, you'll never believe!," Liz gasped right in my face. "Karen got a Christmas present from a guy."

What? That was just not done. "What kind of gift?" I whispered.

"It's an album!"

Noooo. An album? She wasn't even going steady with anyone. "Who gave it to her?" The answer seemed to echo in the room — Rick, the new guy.

"It's *Three Dog Night's Greatest Hits*," Nita added reverently as she and Liz eyed the guy in question.

How did that happen? Since when did guys give such cool gifts? But of course it was from Rick. The recently-transferred-to-our-school guy. He was not your normal transfer kid. His dad drove a Corvette, the kid's hair was always combed and he didn't smell like the guys' locker room. I think he was from Dan Diego or somewhere.

Okay, this night was not looking promising. And there was still THE WALK to get through. See, the walk was the whole reason many kids came to the party. It was a way to get out from under the parental watch and be on our own…in the dark.

THE WALK was a Christmas caroling trek down a lonely country road that lead to one house —Miss M's. There, we would sing every Christmas song we knew.

Now, Miss M was 80- or maybe 90-something. I don't know just how old, but she'd been old my whole life. She had a crackly voice; in fact, she could have been a stereotypical witch if she hadn't always been so nice, serving rocky road candy. And she was one of the few people in town shorter than me — she was tiny. So tiny that when she drove her old black and white Buick from like the 50s, people said all you could see was the steering wheel and two gloved hands.

Yep, she was small but she had guts. Or at least I always thought she did because of her house. Miss M was the granddaughter of a Confederate doctor and still lived in the house her family had built soon after the end of the war. A house that had never been remodeled in a hundred years. Oh, there was electricity and running water, but those were about the only conveniences.

There was a rock cistern, built half in the kitchen and half outside, a setup they had in case of Indian attacks. Shoes worn by her grandfather were lined up all across the front porch, a dusty monument to her kin. She still had his Confederate uniform tucked away in an old chifforobe. The sitting room wallpaper was peeling like skin after a bad sunburn. There were canes always leaning in the corner covered in dust — one with a top made out of a round bullet taken out of a soldier. The floor was slanted, and creaked. Loose bricks jutted out of the chimney like they were trying to make an escape from a fire.

Living there would have been like living in a museum — a museum at the end of a long, dusty lane.

During daylight the house simply looked abandoned, but at night it took on a life of its own. It seemed to just beg for chains to rattle and hinges to creak. In my mind, anyone who slept in that house…yeah, they had guts.

And this creepy old house was a wonderful destination for us as we headed out on our moon-lit caroling trek. It was just scary enough to capture the attention of teenage boys. And as we had discovered soon into junior high, if the boys were interested the girls were too. Plus, Miss M loved to have us croaking, silly acting teenagers serenade her so much that she always cried when we left.

I'd taken the news of Karen's gift pretty well, I thought, or at least I would have if she hadn't had to take all the girls into her room and make a big deal of it. So it was me who kept bringing up caroling, pushing to begin THE WALK. They finally decided to go just to shut me up. I didn't care.

I still wasn't caring as we walked off the main road onto the tree-lined, winding, one-car caliche lane that lead to Miss M's house; the branches forming an arch overhead that couldn't quite block out the light of the full moon, turning everyone into animated shadows. I was caring even less as the guys would sneak ahead on the road, hide and then jump out and scare the girls. And I really wasn't caring as many of the couples started kissing and making out on the way. How could they stand to kiss guys who made fart noises and threw spit-wads? And Charlie was the one who always threw them. Wouldn't I love to have had several to send his way as he was flirting with Sherry? But, I was not caring so I quick walked to the front of the procession.

We moved from the moonlit road to the dark under a huge canopy of hundred-year-old oak trees, then to the front gate heading to the small, front porch light. "Hey, Minton, you better watch for snakes…or flying spit-wads! Ha, ha!"

Charlie. "Shut up, butt-head!," I yelled, "And start singing something." The group launched in to *Deck the Halls* as I was silently praying Miss M hadn't heard me say "butt-head." However, I was determined to be the first to knock on the door and see Miss M if it was the last thing I did.

Wrong choice of words. Because just as I stepped around the shoes on the porch, from the shadows another pair of shoes emerged, attached to a body holding what I knew to be a shotgun.

"*Quien es?*," a voice behind the gun shouted, his face in shadows. "*Quedar alejado!*"

And so, there I was. Eye-to-eye, with barrel-and-barrel.

"*Llamar a la policia!* Call sheriff," the gun holder yelled. Well, great. I'd lose my head and my decapitated body would be drug to jail. I was not finding much holy in this night.

Out of the corner of my eye I saw a kid running away. I watched his escape become a country ballet as he hit a sagging barbed wire fence, so entangling and cutting himself he began to sound like a lost calf. His bawling seemed a fitting soundtrack to the night. I felt a giggle start but then caught the smell of gun oil.

The rest of group had stopped singing. A gun tends to blast the jolly right out of people. The air in our lungs seemed to be sucked right into the bullet chamber. We had all stopped singing at the same time and our minds seemed to register at the same time that Miss M was not here. And then the whispers began...

"Something's happened to Miss M."

"This gun owner has done something to her."

A teenage vigilante group was forming. And I would end up the first casualty.

"What did you do with Miss M?" Liz shouted, standing securely behind her boyfriend.

"I call sheriff", he said for the 15th time. The cold cut through my jacket and forced my brain to start working. I recognized that voice, though he didn't know me from Adam. It was Shorty Chapa. Yep. A person just tall enough that a rifle held shoulder high would be level with my head.

"*Quedar alejado! Tengo un escopeta de dos cañones!*" I had no clue what he was saying.

"Hey, I know some Spanish." Charlie. There were subdued chuckles all around 'til the hammer click of the rifle got everyone's attention.

"I'm serious," Charlie said. "We had some guys fix our fence and they taught me."

I could guess what he learned from the workers. Words junior high kids giggled about. Words that would cause the gun to go off. If that happened, I swore I would come back as a giant spit-wad and crush Charlie flat.

"*Jesu de Cristo. Feliz Navidad*," Charlie called. Shorty tilted his head, the moonlight glimmering off his glasses. In that moment I realized it was all up to him.

I didn't have any control. I hadn't uttered a word since he put me in his sights. Because it really didn't matter what I said if Shorty didn't understand or agree. A lot of things were like that. We could sing Christmas greetings and glad tidings all we wanted...but we couldn't force someone to accept it. You were only responsible for how you handled yourself. And maybe Christmas was simply a reminder that if you wanted good will toward men, you had to *be* good will towards men.

Of course that was the moment one man decided to test my good will. Charlie. He decided to expand on his role as interpreter and made a move toward Shorty. "Hey, man, *juevos de dios...y vaca...*

de caca," said Charlie.

Silence.

Then there was a snort from behind me on the right and a snicker to my left.

Silence.

"Man, did you just say something about eggs and cow poop?" asked one guy.

"Oh my god," gasped Nita, and without thinking I looked over at her, saw her grab her crotch and run to the bushes crying, "I'm gonna pee my pants."

I'm not sure which happened first, Nita peeing her pants because she was laughing so hard, or the gun blast. But suddenly there was a deafening roar and distant screams. Screams I contributed to, though they seemed to echo round and round in my head. Someone grabbed my shirt sleeve and turned me around and away from the blast. Charlie. He seemed to be trying to tell me something and pull me with him but I couldn't hear a thing. He turned around and ran into a rose bush.

As I stared around in the ringing silence, I saw a passed out kid being half carried out of the yard. I could see kids running down the road, one running smack into a tree — I think it was Rick, which gave me a deep down satisfaction — another fell over a pile of rocks, another took a wind chime to the head, still another kid got clotheslined by a grape vine hanging from a tree. They were all eerily lit up by lights—headlights—heading towards us.

Charlie got untangled from the rose bush and stood by me. Nita joined us, her pants darker in some places, as we watched the lights bounce along, herding the running kids back to the house.

The old black and white Buick pulled to a stop. Two little gloved hands. Miss M, alive and well.

By the time my hearing returned, the scene was like one from *Gone with the Wind* where the wounded soldiers are laid out in the center of town for as far as the camera could see. There were kids on benches, on the ground, on the porch, in lawn chairs, many munching on rocky road candy as Miss M passed out band-aids, and bags of ice.

We learned that Shorty was watching over Miss M's place until she returned from her cousin's. She had returned earlier than planned — good thing for us. He was armed because he was scared and the gun blast didn't take my head off because Shorty was laughing so hard at Charlie's stupid spanish, he let the gun slip and accidentally shot a hole in the porch floor.

As the last piece of rocky road candy was finished we managed to regroup and sing a Christmas carol and give hugs to Miss M. She cried as usual. Then we started walking home, a bandaged, bleeding, strangely silent Christmas good-will brigade.

Nita and Charlie and I were bringing up the rear, silent except for Nita's squishing shoes.

"Were you scared?" Charlie asked.

"Scared you were gonna get me shot," I answered.

"I saved your life."

"You throw spit-wads at me."

"Just to get your attention," he quietly said. "Wanna share some spit?"

"Gross!"

And at that point, Nita took off again to the bushes.

MY PATH
(A PRAYER)

Salli Smith

Open the constricted pathway.

Let my heart give love and accept it, freely.

Send me out on my pilgrimage.

Allow my uniqueness to blossom.

To inspire and be inspired.

To drink in the awesome beauty of creation.

To rejoice, with thanksgiving, my life as I know it.

Send me where I must go.

Let peace and acceptance-with-joy guide my path.

Omit procrastination from my being.

Let each moment be utilized as a moment for Thee.

Enrich my soul with Thy Holy Spirit.

Let Your Name be glorified.

Intercede for me, that I may serve You.

Dwell in me, that I may share You.

Let all my fears be replaced by Your love.

Help me to trust that You are leading me.

Walk with me, for I need Your strength and guidance.

Allow hope, hope in You, to reign in my heart,

Today and always.

Amen.

FLY AWAY HOME

Joan Carson

There are several pieces in this book which speak to the incredible sacrifice paid by countless young men and women in the armed services. We do not thank them often enough, and we seldom empathize with the enormity of their commitment. In this memoir, Joan Carson shares her recollections of the longest, loneliest trip of her life.

"What will I find in this big manila envelope?" I thought as the officer handed me the package. He said it contained my husband's personal items. There was the shiny chrome pencil with its four colors of lead. The class ring, intact but so bent out of shape by the impact, told its own story. The little pocket notebook, twisted and with evidence of being slightly warped by moisture, held the notes of dreams, inspiration and vision. Lists of possible future business plans had a section, as did inspirational quotes and a record of flying time.

It all began just a week and a half before. On that Saturday a large typhoon had come across the island of Iwo Jima. It left nearly total destruction. When we came home that night, my husband, Lt. Vern Watson, had phoned operations office. His squadron was assigned to airlift supplies from Japan to Iwo the next morning. He was to navigate one of two C-124 planes. Usually he would as soon fly as eat. He loved it. However, this night his response was different. He didn't want to fly the next day. That was the first time I had seen this attitude in him. It frightened me and I felt like I had knots in my stomach. It's strange that we didn't talk about his unusual reaction.

The next morning he kissed us good-bye and went whistling down the sidewalk with his usual assertive gait. I wanted to run after him and beg him not to go. But then, it was ridiculous to think that way. "Didn't I resolve my anxiety about Vern flying before he entered Air Force cadets? Why am

I doubting God's provision after nearly four years of his career?"

As often happened on a Sunday, the electrical power was to be shut off so that some base repairs could be made. That meant that we couldn't cook and would have no heat in the house. Several of us gals and our children ate lunch at the Officers' Club. Some of the other men that were there walked by our table as they left and jokingly asked if we were "Sunday Widows". This was a term used when desk jockey husbands were getting their flying time in on the weekend. But this time those words made me shudder and my insides churn.

That afternoon, the only way to keep warm on the cloudy, cold November day was to crawl in bed. I put our one-year-old daughter, Robin, down in her crib for a nap. As I snuggled under the blankets in my bed, it was more than the cold house that made me shiver. In spite of everything, I did go to sleep. Suddenly at 1700 I was awakened with a start and jumped out of bed. What was happening? I knew that something was wrong. Again I calmed down, but all of the accumulated experiences and feelings of the day couldn't be erased. At about 1900, I decided to call Operations about Vern's expected return time.

The only phone available to our base neighborhood was outside. My footsteps halted in front of the light pole where the red box protected a telephone. I shivered as I pulled the sweater around my body. The baby was unusually quiet inside my nearly seven month pregnant uterus. A strange feeling of dread gripped me as I slowly opened the box.

"Oh God, no! This is Sunday. The squadron adjutant shouldn't be answering the phone!" With mouth dry and throat tight, I asked Capt. Spironi what Vern's ETA would be. The background sounds of airplane engines revving and voices loudly giving directives were inappropriate for the office on a Sunday evening.

Suddenly Col. Jackson was saying, "Would you like to speak with me?"

"Oh no! He shouldn't be there," I thought, "and why would I need to speak to the commanding officer? Oh God, something's happened to Vern."

I felt that my knees were giving way beneath me.

"Mrs. Watson, their plane crashed after take-off at Iwo Jima. It was only at an estimated 100-feet altitude when it dived into the jungle. There was one survivor. He was not a crew member…Are you alone?…We will send someone to be with you," the colonel said with obvious tightness in his voice. I don't remember what else he told me except that the chaplain would be coming out to see me. I heard myself saying, "I have friends nearby. Thank you." I replaced the phone and closed the door on the red box.

I stood there trembling in the cold, damp night air. Afraid to take a step. It seemed as if my legs were numb. I couldn't make myself move. I felt nauseated and weak and so very much alone. What should I do? Robin was in the house asleep but I couldn't make myself go back in there. I needed to find someone to be with me. It was only a few steps to Mildred and Keith Tester's home. I still don't know how I made it over there, walked into the patio and tapped on the sliding glass door. When Mildred saw me she gasped "What's happened?" and I spilled out the story as Col. Jackson had given it to me.

Mildred and another friend, Helen, spent the evening with me. Helen stayed the night. There were so many things to do. It seems strange, but we had to make lists and get organized immediately. I don't remember if I shed a tear while they were there or if it is was when I had gone to bed and was all alone. I grabbed Vern's pillow and buried my face in it. I kept hearing his words: "I want us to be interdependent. Independent when you have to be and leaning on each other when we're together." And I sobbed and sobbed until there were no more tears. The sadness was so profound that it went beyond any expression with weeping or words.

Often during the following days I thought about the fact that, just a few months before his death, we had spent a wonderful week in the mountains with missionary friends. Vern shared with me that he had surrendered to the Lord for full-time service.

"So, God, how do you plan to accomplish this now? We know he's praising you full-time in heaven, but what about here on earth? Just what is your plan?" thought my questioning heart.

One of the groups of army men near our base had invited the chaplain's family to join them for Thanksgiving Dinner at their mess hall. Robin and I were included in the invitation. What an experience that was. So many young men in a foreign land on a holiday, away from family and home. They were finding comfort in giving us comfort. Many of them had younger brothers and sisters or children of their own. It was a joy for them to have Hal's daughters and my Robin with them. Our children were the main attraction. The decorations were festive and the food was excellent. It was the most memorable Thanksgiving that I've experienced. This whole group was family for me . . . and our children brought joy to them and eased their loneliness.

The next week a memorial service took place at the large base chapel. After shopping, packing and saying good-byes, Robin and I were returning to the United States. Lt. Jean Carson, and his wife, Virginia, were to serve as our military escort. They were rotating back to the States for another assignment and would travel with us as far as California. What an exhausting trip, confined to a plane for three legs of 12 hours each. We arrived at Travis Air Force Base in the middle of the night, went to quarters to sleep and didn't get up until midday. I was amazed at Robin's adaptation to this trip—no fussing—just sort of in shock and in awe of what was happening to us. Oh yes, she had enjoyed her first Spanish omelet.

Our flight to Des Moines, Iowa, departed San Francisco at 6:45 p.m. that day. One stop was scheduled for Omaha, Nebraska. The Carsons flew to their home in Texas later that evening. I felt some apprehension about traveling alone with Robin. The weather predictions of a cold front had not been reassuring. Early in the flight the plane soared into turbulence. An elderly gentleman and I were given oxygen masks by the stewardess since we had been experiencing labored breathing. All of the other passengers were writhing, retching and making use of the airsick bags. What a mess! This raging storm was presenting a challenge for everyone. An announcement from the pilot informed us that we were to make an unscheduled stop in Denver. After landing, every passenger was directed to leave the plane. We waited in the terminal while the entire plane interior was cleaned. Wind was blowing the heavy snow and we wondered how our trip might deviate from the flight plan.

We boarded the plane and took off for our destination. Little did we know what the hours ahead would hold for us. As we were flying over Nebraska, icing became a threat. The cold front had blown in with fury and brought a sudden temperature drop. An announcement informed us the flight would be grounded at Omaha. All of us were anxious, frustrated and wondering how we could consider travel with conditions so treacherous. Quickly we learned that we'd be hustled over to the terminal and loaded into buses. It made no sense at all to endanger our lives in a bus sliding all over the icy highway.

The Des Moines terminal was dingy and dimly lit, empty except for a couple of shabbily dressed men. Trying to find shelter from the bitter cold Iowa weather? Vagrants? The stale smell of cigarette stubs filled the air. It took every ounce of strength to move the suitcases across the floor, pushing them with my foot. First one and then the other. Here and there loose linoleum tiles redirected or toppled one of the Samsonite bags. Oh, how I yearned for the warmth of family. They were nowhere in sight.

Why? Why weren't they there? Didn't they get the message? Maybe they didn't know that this is where we'd arrive. What do I do now? If they aren't here, where are they? If they did not receive the message in time, the airport would be their destination. If they did go there, they would know that our flight was cancelled in Omaha. Were they told that we were hustled onto a bus to travel over icy roads to Des Moines?

Again and again my mind cried ,"Oh God! I feel so frightened. Help me to be strong for my babies".

I cuddled my sleeping little girl and held her close. A heavy sigh grew into a silent sob that shook my body. The diaper bag and the big pigskin shoulder bag were still draped over my shoulders. Exhaustion and stress had left me drained mentally and physically. Gradually I found energy to be aware of dismal surroundings and assess our circumstances.

It was obvious Mom and Daddy had not received the information that we would be here at the bus depot. Would they go back home? Not without having accurate information of the whereabouts of their daughter and granddaughter. Never would they imagine that buses would attempt to travel on highways covered with a coating of ice. Their friends live about an hour's drive up the road if they headed home. I knew they'd stop there.

It was comforting to hear that soft familiar "Hello".

"Esther?"

"Yes, your folks are here".

What relief in Mother's words when she knew that we had arrived safely. They had been misinformed at the airport when told that our flight was grounded in Denver. She was appalled that a bus sliding over the miles of icy roads was the alternative.

This account needs to close with some of the inspirational quotes written in Vern's notebook.

"...It was not the outer grandeur of the Roman but the inner simplicity of the Christian that lived on through the ages." — Charles A. Lindbergh

"...give vent to the spirit of adventure which learns to control fear." — Grantly Dick Read, M.D.

"We do not create power. We just utilize it." — FeamCom Chaplain

"It is impossible to argue with a liar, and the devil is a liar." — Mr. Pape

"I shall find a way or make one." — Robert E. Perry

A ONE MAN BAND

Denise Fitch

Not all sermons are delivered in church. Some are found in hospitals, in committee meetings, in conversations on an airplane…you might even hear one, as Denise Fitch did, from a street corner musician.

Walking to the bus stop after work, I hear a familiar sound in the distance. As I get closer, I realize it from someone who is "a one man band."

As I reach the bus stop, I watch him from across the street. My heart fills with sadness for him and I want to do something for him. It is a sound that I've heard before, a man wearing a contraption strapped to his back, connected to his feet in a way that he can make music and be "a one man band". As he moves his feet in a dancing manner, it pulls the straps to play the drums and cymbals. At the same time, he sings and plays the banjo and, when he is not singing, he is playing the harmonica. He reminds me of a wind-up toy that plays the cymbals and dances. I know that he hopes that people will stop and enjoy his music and in appreciation of his music they will toss money in his banjo case, but it's not working that way today.

From what I can see from across the street, he looks like a man in his 60s, he looks a little scruffy. He could use a shave and his clothes are worn. As he sings, I hear that he has a nice soothing voice with a touch of Irish ,and the music he plays sounds upbeat and fun. I realize the reason why he is on the street playing is to bring a smile and some joy to those who pass by and listen and perhaps make some money. The first time I saw him, he had a crowd gathered around him and everyone was enjoying his music, but today there is no crowd around him, no one to show their appreciation, not today.

I know that what he is doing right now might not be what he really wants to do; he does it to survive. I believe people should be able to live their life with dignity and respect, not have to beg for money to survive, to be able to live in a way so they can feel productive and useful and not do something out of desperation.

All of us should appreciate and be grateful for all the many blessings we have in our lives, but we should also help others around us to live a more productive and meaningful life by showing them grace and love. We often take for granted people or things in our life that are most dear to us and we could so easily lose in a blink of an eye. As our lives change direction—not always for the good—we must make choices, sometimes good ones and sometimes bad ones and it takes us a while to get back on track. Sometimes we spend so much time worrying about the future; that we miss what God has planned for us today. For those that are on a not-so-good track, let us open our hearts with kindness and help with our resources. We don't know who might be that person who needs that kind word or hug or even a helping hand. It could be a stranger or it could be someone you know or it could even be a friend. We all need someone in the world to be there for us; maybe we can start today.

It hurts my heart to see and hear him trying so hard to please those that walk by, putting himself out there to be made fun of or to be ridiculed. Why? Because he has fallen on bad times, or he's lost his job and his confidence? Or perhaps it's that he is older, can't find a job and this is what he has to do to survive. He may feel that his time has come and gone and that things are better left to the younger generation. There is a part of me that would like to think that what he is doing is because he loves to perform, to make people smile, that this is something he's always wanted to do and now he has the chance and he is not just doing this for the money. But I know in my heart that that is probably not the case. Sometimes in life we may all have to do things we never dreamed we'd ever have to do, something that is beneath us or degrading, but we do it because we have to. Wouldn't it be wonderful to have someone to help you through the tough times? I would hope that we would all have compassion for those going through hard times and would reach out to them with love and grace in our own way. Maybe today you can start showing that love and grace to those around you.

We are all put on this earth for a purpose until the time comes when we go to be with the Father in eternity. And maybe our purpose right now is to bring joy to those around us by playing music for others to enjoy or for others to tell us their story through their music. Maybe today we can start to love each other, maybe today.

GREEN BANANAS

By Gloria Gene Moore

While memoirs of a journey (or two, or three) through a bout with cancer can easily lapse into depressing monotony or self-pity, Gloria's cancer story manages to be uplifting, optimistic and forward-looking.

I've had three gut-wrenching journeys in Cancerland and, each time, I've bounced back stronger with my faith in God and in my body's ability to heal itself, fortified by Mysterious Powers I will never understand.

My adventures in Cancerland started thirty-one years ago at the tender age of twenty-seven when I was diagnosed with Hodgkin's Disease. In the 1970's, finding a "cure" for Hodgkin's was one of the first major victories in President Nixon's War on Cancer.

Back then, ten times more radiation was used than it is now, and I, like many of my fellow soldiers from those early victories in the war on cancer, ended up with additional treatment-related cancers. Twenty-three years after my initial treatment, mine showed up in the form of matching tumors in both breasts, right outside the fields of the original radiation. This was devastating news to a former teenage South Texas beauty queen who paid her way through college twirling fire batons and machetes!

Double mastectomies and reconstruction followed, only for me to have my life disrupted seven years later by an even more deadly form of cancer that erupted in the tissue that was spared from which my gorgeous new breasts were reconstructed.

It took MD Anderson three biopsies to figure out what was going on. When I learned I had angiosarcoma of the breast, a breast cancer so rare it constitutes less than .02 percent of all breast cancers, I Googled it. The prognosis was grim. The average survival rate for my Stage III diagnosis was less than 24% for living for 17 months or more from the time of diagnosis.

I decided to do everything in my power to assist God in putting me in that 24%. I radically changed my diet, stepped up my exercise plan and did a great deal of spiritual searching about what I would do for my remaining time on the planet.

In contemplating my unfinished business, I finally acknowledged that the altar call tug I felt as a teenager when attending my local fundamentalist Baptist church was now propelling me to make a professional avocation of all the volunteer work I had been doing to help newly-diagnosed people navigate their journeys. For the past four years, I have, as a volunteer, coordinated Riverbend's cancer support group. This, along with my volunteer work with other cancer advocacy causes, has put me in touch with many newly-diagnosed people with all types of cancers at every varying stage. I found myself praying over the phone and in person with total strangers and loved the sacredness of our connections, even in the most devastating circumstances.

My spiritual journey has led me from a black-and-white view of God to a place of embracing the Mysteries of a Higher Power. After getting extremely mad at God over my original diagnosis and after years of asking, "why me?", I came to a place of Grace. I now fully realize that humans can be healed and whole, even when the external circumstances appear otherwise. Amazingly, this has given me a Peace that Passes Understanding, even in the middle of all of my medical uncertainties. As I have watched countless others move through cancer treatment and other seriously grave health conditions, I have come to realize that the spiritual walk through these challenges is more important to most people than any type of medical treatment.

While undergoing my most recent series of chemotherapy, I did a great deal of soul searching. I kept asking myself what was it I hadn't done yet in my life that I would regret not having done if my life were to end right then. The idea of going to seminary kept popping up. The altar call of my childhood kept rearing its head like the pop-ups in the carnival game of Whack-A-Mole. I decided if I made it, I wanted to spend whatever time I had left on this planet helping others who were also trying to transform their Dark Nights of the Soul, aka cancer experiences and health challenges, into spiritual wisdom. I decided the right way for me to answer God's call to this work was to become a chaplain.

I started looking for a chaplaincy training program that would accept someone at my age with my medical history and found one of the only masters degree programs in chaplaincy in the country was located right here in Austin, Texas.

My plan appeared brutally interrupted, when at my first four-month checkup after completing fourteen grueling months of chemo, the scans and Xrays revealed what looked for sure like a metastasis of angiosarcoma in a deadly location, right between my lungs and my spine.

My oncologist encouraged me have surgery immediately to see if the "something" could be removed because more chemo and radiation were no longer options for me. I've met my lifetime limits. Meanwhile, my husband and I prepared ourselves for my impending journey of transition into whatever follows our time in this world.

The surgeon recommended he do a biopsy before heading straight to surgery, and rescheduled the surgery for five days after the biopsy.

I woke up from the fog of the biopsy to an interventional radiation technician smiling at me, telling me, "Ma'am, you are a lucky gal. When the biopsy needle went in, a lot of green goo drained out. Cancer doesn't drain. Its solid. We will send the sample off to the lab to see if there were any cancer cells in what came out but I've worked here 15 years and I doubt there will be any."

He had to repeat this story three times before I could comprehend what he was saying. My life changed in a flash. The attending nurse had tears in her eyes as she wheeled me into the recovery area. "This is a wonderful and amazing outcome," she said. "We don't get days like this as often as we'd like. Your scans sure looked like another angiosarcoma."

Though I will never get the medical authorities to call it one, I'm claiming this as my miracle. I truly believe this was a divine intervention. I believe I've been spared to complete my unfinished business and after 40 years of wandering in the wilderness of other careers, to at long last answer that altar call.

Providence being what it is, I have just completed my first year of a three year program at Austin's Seminary of the Southwest leading to a masters degree and board certification in Chaplaincy and Pastoral Care.

I'll be at most people's retirement age by the time I graduate. I can't help but smile when people look at me incredulously for starting this journey at a time in my life when most folks at my age and with my medical history wouldn't even buy green bananas.

I tell them, thirty-two years ago I was a young-adult cancer survivor, and thanks to God and God-inspired developments in modern medicine, I'm now an almost senior citizen-cancer survivor with a brand new and wonderful future in front of me.

I live with the wonderful grace of knowing that we are never too old, too sick, or too whatever to keep from doing whatever great idea it is that God has planted in our hearts.

ORIGIN OF A POEM

Darwyn Hanna

We often have guest authors speak to our SCRIBE group. Darwyn says that this poem was inspired by an author's description of his creative work habits.

Lord, giving me a poem to express how I feel
Is like going fishing without a rod or reel.
Leave the safety of the shore to feel the power of the deep;
Fill my mind with good thoughts before I nod off to sleep.

The subconscious mind is always at work;
It organizes in our sleep, a blessing of a perk.
I just ride the tide in anything that'll float
And wait for the fish to jump in the boat.

The subconscious mind, a miracle in action,
Cultivated consciously, reveals creative traction.
Fed by the wheels of research for a poem on demand,
Allowed to simmer and incubate, it comes out to beat the band.

Coached by life experience, it surfaces by surprise,
Usually in the morning, FREE — but what a prize.
The subconscious mind, God's creative workshop:
Give it a try, you may never stop.

OLD FRIENDS

Bob Moore

You'd like another serving from Bob Moore? I can't blame you. Try this one and remember that right now you're older than you've ever been in your life. And now you're even older.

In my youth—meaning younger than fifty—I knew old people the way one knows people from Peru. That is to say, intellectually and stereotypically. I knew old people the way most of us know those of a different generation. They might as well have been aliens. The elderly were not like the rest of us. They dwelt in the past, in a meaningless place and time. When I was young, I thought of oldsters as having outlived their usefulness, graybeards who, although they might once have lived and loved as I had witnessed in old movies, no longer had relevance. They suffered the inevitable aches and pains, they reminisced endlessly about the good old days, and they listened ad nauseum to the music of the fifties. Sooner rather than later, they would require someone to keep the oil changed on their wheel chair. At least, that's what I thought then.

As I said, I know old people—much better now than I used to. I had my weekly lunch with one of them on Thursday. As we entered the restaurant, Ray—bent over, stooped like a character from Dickens and using a cane—had his eyes fixed firmly on the floor. He has fallen frequently of late and not long ago had to be taken to the emergency room at four a.m., bleeding from a gash on his head. But now we were in his favorite hamburger joint. The waiter was solicitous with just a tinge of pity in his voice. The other customers, all under thirty, probably expected us to order a bowl of warm milk in which to dip our toast.

They saw us as old people, which of course, we are, measured chronologically. But they couldn't know how we saw each other. I can't speak for Ray, but here is what I saw across the table. I saw a tennis player who refused to be beaten; a prankster who loved the practical joke; a learned professor, author and teacher who is still revising the eleventh edition of his textbook. We talked, not about the good old days and not even about the feckless behavior of youth, but about an upcoming real estate development and the race for governor. We discussed his garden and how to keep birds from pecking the tomatoes and when we might hit golf balls at the driving range. We even admired a passing waitress. I like to think our conversation could have been held by someone thirty years younger than we.

Ray is hump-backed and slow now. I don't like to admit it, but I am not as fast as I used to be, either. But we remain friends, laughing at the same old jokes and enjoying each other's company.

I like my friend Ray. He is old now—just south of ninety. His mind races ahead, however, just as it always has. It's hard to keep up with him. I like all my friends – young and old. The young keep me interested in life, but the old remind me of how interesting life can become. That's why I like my friends—all of my friends. But old friends are to be especially treasured. One of these days I will get around to thanking each of them personally for their friendship.

Unless of course, I don't remember to.

FACES

Deborah Rose

Deborah Register writes poetry under the name Deborah Rose…an especially fitting surname, given the topic of this blossoming poem.

What was before I do not know.
I just was, then began to grow.
For grow we must, or die, no choice,
No in-between, a dreamless sleep or life rejoice.

Pressed, compressed, buried dark as night,
I struggled, pained, strained toward the light,
Never stopping, popping through, encouraged by the rain,
'Til tiny tendrils danced and daylight's delight I gain.

Where I am know not I,
A timid, peeking, seeking spy.
A wonderland!
A garden grand!
A royal court of every hue!
Surely 'tis Eden I've come into!

Hiding small and still, the unseen one,
I gaze amazed at everyone.
Oh! Queen Rose, you sensual treat,
Let me bow before your feet!
Forever reign in dignity!
Oh, may I grow a rose to be!

Who's in that place,
The one with such a smiling face,
Brightly, boldly, bursting gay?
Why, 'tis Daisy greets and graces day.
Would I, could I, dream higher
Than its golden, glowing glory aspire?

Look there!
Could any in all of life compare?
Lavender, Lily, Lilac, share
A lovely tender violet hue.
That's it. Nothing less for me will do.

Behold! See proudly parading by the wall
Soldiers strutting straight and tall,
Heralds proclaiming "Spring!" in pastel.
Tulip trumpets "All is well".
What higher calling could I ask
Than to apply myself to tulip's task?

Perhaps the popular Marigold,
Happily humming has instead foretold
My future, blessing busy bees
Porting pollen up to their knees.

While in this august court I bask,
I cannot help myself but ask
Will I grow to be so fine?
Which perfection is destined mine?
And so I slumber in summer's silent sun,
Unseen yet by anyone.

Then it began quite unexpected.
Unformed, unseen, not yet respected,
My tiny tendrils outed!
Without even trying, my parts have sprouted!

Curling, unfurling, my petals unfold!
Gasp! What a horrid creature I behold!
All spiky yellow little daggers pointing.
I have none of the garden's graceful anointing.

An interloper, an uninvited guest,
No doubt despised by all the rest.
Haughty taunting comes my reception,
Nothing less and no exception.

Bending low and feeling small,
Invisible I pray beside the wall.
No rose for me. No daffodil.
Unless…Unless…Yes! I will!
I will be a rose! I will try and try!
I will be a rose or I will die!

Obey my will! My power is felt!
All my yellow daggers melt!
Holding tightly to that thought
My transfiguration is actually wrought.

Those daggers now rosebuds I truly see,
And in the morning the queen sees me!
"How lovely you grow!" she compliments.
"Thank you!" I blush for the grace she sent.
I smile with my secret struggle inside.
A rose out there and me inside.

Now Daisy is silent and turns her head.
"She dislikes your rose" my inner voice said.
Deciding to take the next bud in hand,
I squeezed and teased 'til 'twas daisy gold and grand!
She smiled. "Good morning to you." I replied.
Only I knew that to Rose and Daisy I lied.

Next I made the purplest purple I knew how,
Then I stood tall and took a bow.
All the purple petaled pals cheered "Wow!"
Next, forming my tulip ('twas extremely hard),
I greeted saluting heralds in the yard.

But as my blossoms increase my grip gets weak.
And the acceptance and praise that I earnestly seek,
Seems to be shifting and drifting, with each new attempt.
My greetings seem meeted with curious contempt.

This may not be the best plan I laid,
Putting on this tired masquerade.
Can I put aside this game I've made?
Can I stop this sad, endless, exhausting charade?
Can I let go that will that molds each face?
I have lost myself! They have taken my place!

The friends I had I now sorely lack.
I hear them talking behind my back.
"What kind of friend is that?" they say,

"Different to everyone, daisy then and rose today."
"He has too many faces! A friend indeed!"
'Tis surely a new beginning I need.

With relief and remorse within I seek
Myself, my truth, and I "untweak".
One by one faux faces lose their fake grin.
I turn to the sun and soak it in.

Now yellow daggers spike up form their places.
No rose, no daisy, no tulip, no other graces
My branches, my stems, my one true bower.
No. Now I embrace my unique wildflower.

Alas! Who is this now that comes to court?
A glorious form, a different sort!
She sings as she passes along ordered rows,
Sweet melodies pruning as she goes.
Trimming, nipping, clipping, even amputating!
Each courtier looks ecstatic awaiting
Her embrace and improving attentions,
Handmade magic, her intentions.

The gardener perfects each petal, blade, and stem,
With the beautiful harmony only heard in a hymn.
Her sweet song and tender touch
Convince me she loves them each so very much.

She's drawing near now and I cower in fear,
Will she see I'm an unplanned interloper here?
What a disappointment! What unwanted fruit!
Surely she'll grasp me, discard me, dagger, stem, and root!

Alas! Her dazzling gaze upon me has lighted!
But instead of disdain, her expression's delighted!
""Look! Just what my garden's needed," says she.
I can hardly believe she's speaking of me.
"Very unique, you brave little blossom."
"Of all of my flowers I think you're the top one!"

My heart be still! Her grace made me see
That all I needed to be was me.

SHADOWS OF JOY

Joan Costello

We write out of joy. We write out of pain. We write to share. We write to purge. In many cases, we write because we have to, because we hope to find answers. Joan Costello finds meaning in an event which could seem merely mean.

If God had said, "Larry and Joan, I am going to answer your prayer request for a child of your own, but you must promise to give him back after a couple of years", our answer would have been no. Yet we would not have wished that this experience had not happened to us.

After 13 years of trying to have a child of our own, we were so excited to hear the pregnancy test was positive. We were happy nurturing our good looking intelligent, healthy and active 11-year old son, Michael, who was 14-months old when we adopted him in England years before.

The overwhelming joy of hearing the first cry of this healthy little boy who looked just like his father, from the reddish blond hair…right down to the long, skinny legs.

We were an Air Force family in Austin, Texas, but we were assigned to be in Alaska just days after man's first walk on the moon in July 1969. Due to Timmy's birth, Larry received a two month deferment. Unbeknownst to me, this was the first of many gifts of grace bestowed by God through the AF. ("By Grace are you saved through faith, and not of ourselves, for it is the gift of God" —Ephesians 2:8.)

October 1969 in Fairbanks Alaska was unseasonably warm and pleasant, and I was able to carry

Timmy for many a long walk that first month we were in a hotel waiting for Base Housing.

In November, just as the snow and sub-zero weather hit, Timmy began to run high fevers and had trouble holding down fluids. Just after Thanksgiving, Timmy was admitted to our tiny Air Force hospital for a series of blood tests, bone marrow examination and spinal tap. Two weeks before Christmas, our young pediatrician called us into his office to tell us the results of the tests. It seemed Timmy's were similar to leukemia cells, yet unlike any of the charted leukemia family of cells. He would call us back when a firm diagnosis could be made. With a slim ray of hope, we left the hospital and returned to the bustle of the holidays with a sinking feeling in the pit of our stomachs.

The dark January afternoon in Alaska became even darker, as we shivered in disbelief in our Air Force pediatrician's hot office. We learned that Neimann-Pick is a genetic fat storage disease which had invaded Timmy's liver and spleen.

We learned that Larry and I were both carriers of this rare disease, even though we were told the chances of two carriers marrying is one in 80,000. We had no history of anything like this in either of our Protestant Midwestern families. This and other similar type metabolic disorders, such as Tay Sacks, are not known as a Christian disease. They mainly appear in Jewish children. We were told that Timmy probably would not live to see his third birthday.

After Larry returned to work, that same January afternoon became even darker and bleaker, until an Air Force chaplain came to see me. We had met his wife and six healthy children—five of them boys—the first day in Alaska. Larry had told him our devastating news and Chaplain Lantz felt he had to come visit me right away. He just listened with a perceptible "agape" love as I poured out my broken heart. I believe God sends us people. Later this chaplain, who hosted a weekly Christian radio program at the local North Pole Alaska station, asked me to read a poem I had written for Timmy, which later was used by the 1971 March of Dimes:

> They shy away.
> They do not know what to say
> To this child who cannot talk or play.
> Yet he speaks to them through and through
> With eyes so big and blue.
> Is there something you might do
> To help me walk and talk like you?"

Bob introduced me to Keith Miller and other Christian authors who helped me in my spiritual growth. He also encouraged me to write about Timmy for therapy. His wife Nancy, a creative artist, made a master mug mold for me which introduced me to the Ceramics Shop on base. Although shut in during the long dark Alaska winter, I had books, writing, ceramics, and Timmy to keep me sane since I did not have an opportunity to make many new friends. Sometimes Michael watched his little brother on a moonlight night, while Larry and I rode away with The Ripple Riders. Several of us couples took to the snowmobile trails with a small bottle of cheap Ripple wine in our pockets and we would stop for refreshment while watching the aurora borealis sweep down around us.

February found Timmy and me winging our way to Johns Hopkins Research Hospital in Baltimore, aboard a C141 air evacuation hospital plane which stopped to refuel in Anchorage, on its way from Japan to Washington, D.C. It was midnight as Timmy and I were rushed by Air Force ambulance onto the snowy flight line and hustled aboard the waiting plane.

I forced a smile to match Timmy's as I carried him down one of two long aisles lined with stretchers stacked three-deep on each side of us. Not having been briefed beforehand, I was quite surprised to find that Timmy and I were the only dependents on a planeload of casualties from the Vietnam battlefields. After landing in Washington, some of us disembarked to a waiting bus, while others were put aboard ambulances and some aboard hearses.

After two weeks of thorough diagnostic testing at Johns Hopkins Hospital, I had a conclusive interview with a renowned genetic research professor of pediatrics, giving me the ultimate results of their findings. I was ready for what I was told, but how could I accept the fact that this child—this child that I loved so much, that I had waited for so long to hold, this child who is the image of his adoring father—will have a very short, unhealthy future. The tears came silently, as I returned to Timmy's and my room, shared with two other mothers and babies. Timmy and I were quite seasoned travelers by the time we returned to Alaska, and our family tried to live a somewhat normal life. It felt good to be back in snow with my sheepskin parka which had me smelling like a wet sheep during the D.C. rains. Also it was good not to be awakened in the middle of the night by the "wolf pack" as we mothers called the interns who woke us and our babies as they poked and talked about their disease in this renowned research hospital.

After his sixth month, Timmy had a gradual loss of muscle tone in his perfectly formed body. With a pure, lovable, happy personality, he held one's attention with his beautiful eyes. These clear angelic eyes, which pierced one through and through, were the source of many poems, one beautifully expressed by a young pilot who came to know Timmy through an Air Force nurse. The strength we received through those eyes helped us to endure the gradual loss of Timmy's eyesight, along with the loss of his mental alertness.

Two weeks before Timmy's second birthday, we were again winging our way to Washington D.C., this time to the National Institute of Health. Timmy had became very fragile and limp. He lost all his muscle tone and he could no longer smile. He quit trying to talk and could only express himself in grunts of pain or pleasure. I recorded Timmy's favorite nursery rhymes and lullaby music and now we traveled with a tape recorder and a few small musical toys, and the stuffed animals that helped support Timmy's back and limbs. The Air Force provided a special bed and a hospital table on which to roll Timmy around on. A medical specialist designed and built a custom recliner chair with a soft synthetic sheepskin rug on which to lay Timmy's fragile body. Again "God sends us people" and" His Grace"

Larry flew down from Alaska to join me in meeting with the N.I.H. research doctors to evaluate the feasibility of trying a new experiment. It had been six weeks since Larry last saw his son. Timmy loved his daddy and relished the time Larry held him. He would curl his perfect little hand around Larry's finger, hold on tight and "talk up a storm" to his dad. The only audible word to escape Timmy's lips was a greeting, "Daddy." Now, other pediatric parents shed tears with us as Larry bent over Timmy's bed to greet his son. It hurt so much to look at him with his leg in a new cast (his bones had become extremely brittle) and so, so thin, lying uncovered because of a low-grade fever. Larry's shoulders shook with great silent sobs because Timmy no longer remembered his daddy.

The N.I.H. was not ready for this experiment and convinced us that if they should try it, and it would work, Timmy's present brain damage was irreparable. A renowned research doctor told me that we could expect Timmy to get much worse, probably to where we would not be able to care for him at home. All I could say at this point was, "I believe in miracles" and he softly answered "I do, too, but I do not count on them." That is when we started living one day at a time. Once again, left with no hope whatsoever, we decided to return to Austin. Larry planned to retire in less than a year, and we left many friends in Texas. Timmy and I flew from D.C. to Austin in an air evacuation plane and Larry and Michael drove the pickup camper down the Alcan highway with a new Siberian Husky puppy.

A top Austin pediatric specialist was assigned to visit us at President Johnson's Presidential Suite at Bergstrom AFB hospital where Timmy and I were housed while waiting for our new house purchase to go through. Gradually, I found myself letting Timmy go. However, I could not let him be placed in some institution where no one could give him the love or care he could get from his family. At that time, I did not realize Timmy's constant care took me away from the rest of my family.

We could no longer hold Timmy's body close to ours or pick him up, for he cried out in pain when he was touched. I could only dress him in loose knit clothing. He once loved for me to hold him up over my shoulder and dance around the room to music. No longer. By his third Christmas, we helplessly watched Timmy lose his eyesight, and mental regression crept in rapidly to prove that the abnormal fat cells were storing in his brain tissue. I came home and cried after passing through the toy department of the Bergstrom AFB exchange. It hurt so much to know Timmy had no use for any of the toys of a normal three-year-old child.

Only once did I cry as I held Timmy. This was when he was not yet a year old and could still move his arms and hands.

There Is No End

It was a most distressing day.
I could only weep when I wanted to pray
For this child who cannot creep or play.
Then cuddling him in all my fears,
A weakened hand appears…
And he brushed away my tears
By softly touching my face…
And his eyes pleaded that day
In a most reassuring way…
As if to say…
"Mommy, everything is OK."

We talked with him, we laughed with him, we kidded with him, and we sympathized with him as if he were a normal, growing child. The shadows of our sorrow were carefully masked in joy in Timmy's presence.

New Years Day 1972 found Timmy in a new leg cast after another bone fracture. He was retaining fluids and his every-other-day suppositories were no longer working. Then Larry's mother, whom he and Timmy resembled, died in Ohio. While we returned from the airport, a friend staying with Timmy had taken a phone call from the N.I.H. They had a treatment for Timmy! We knew it was too late, but upon Larry's return to Texas, Timmy and I left once again for D.C. By now we had friends there who were with me that long week. I was admitted as a patient and shared a room with him. By mid-week, three blood tests for the enzyme experiment were not working and even though no experiment was done to Timmy, he was in a bad state of regression. By Saturday, Timmy seemed to be getting better and possibly by Monday we could return to Texas. As I held him in his sheepskin, and talked to him, even though his doctors said he could not hear, I felt a slight grip from his limp clenched fist I had put around my finger. And a certain sparkle of joy came to his eyes and it came again when I played his music as he fell asleep. I turned off the tape after his favorite, "Brahms Lullaby".

The next morning, our favorite nurse came into the room. After taking Timmy's temperature, she turned to my bed and said, "Mrs. Jackson, I don't think Timmy is with us anymore".

I rushed to Timmy's bed and gently turned him over from his side, where I had placed him during the night. Tears of relief flowed freely as I found, instead of the usual grimace of pain, a slight smile on his face, and he had not been able to smile in months.

A complete autopsy was attended by a Japanese brain specialist who happened to be in D.C. He found that Timmy's hearing was not impaired, as it was generally known to be in this advanced stage of his disease.

Returning home alone, I wrote one last poem for Timmy. It was skillfully read at his funeral by our minister with Brahms Lullaby playing in the background.

Oh Lord, we did not want to let him go,
This child of ours, we loved him so.
Yet we did not want to see him stay
If he could not run and sing and talk and play.
So peaceful he lay…that day…he went away.
Thank you for the joy
Given by this frail little boy
Who came to teach in many a way
That others like him may have a better day.
May the strength that he gave
Continue to teach and to save
You've gone in peace, our little one
You've gone in peace, our precious son."

Yes, Lord, we would not have wished that this experience had not happened to us.

GRANDPA'S CHRISTMAS BLESSINGS

Peter A. Hubbard

Peter's memories of one special Christmas exemplify the impact a small incident can have on a child, the repercussions of which may be felt even decades later.

It was coming up on the Christmas of '58, and I could hardly wait. Being only seven partially explained my impatience. But what would make *this* Christmas extra special for a typically squirmy, farm-raised Wisconsin second-grader was the fact I would be celebrating this Christmas in TEXAS —with ALL FOUR of my Grandparents!

Believe it nor not, I was less interested in the presents I'd get than I was in making the 1,600-mile cross-country December trek down Route 66—away from cold-and-snowy Wisconsin to warm-and-sunny Texas. While I'd spent countless hours exploring my Grandpa and Grandma Hubbard's Wisconsin dairy farm, roaming the barns, fields and pastures almost daily, I was only three years old the last time I last visited Grandpa and Grandma Wipff's turkey farm near Devine, about an hour south of San Antonio.

A natural-born adventurer, I could hardly wait to shadow Grandpa Wipff, and to assist him in taking care of those strange-looking birds—turkeys! Packed like sardines in our shiny new two-tone, blue-and-white '58 Ford station wagon were my parents and my precocious five-year-old sister, Sheila. Joining the trek South were my Wisconsin grandparents—Kenneth and Adelaide—who brought along my still-single-at-27 Aunt Joyce in their two-tone green '53 Buick Special.

The Christmas of '57 had been memorable, too, but for different reasons. It had been spent in the small prairie town of Limon, Colorado, where my dad had pastored his very first church. That year my Wisconsin grandparents had not only come to spend it with us, I had gotten every present a

1950's six-year-old could possibly want.

I can still remember all those goodies nestled under the tree! The biggest package torn open that Christmas morning revealed a brand new Lionel train. It came with a bright red engine and six shiny cars, plus a set of miniature billboards, with really cool advertising on them.

Helping me enjoy more realistic games of Cowboys-and-Indians with the neighbor boys were a shiny pair of six-shooters, complete with leather holsters … *and* a rocking horse, a handsome cowboy hat and tooled cowboy boots! Also nestled under the tree that year, provided by my Texas grandparents, was my very own Davy Crockett bedspread—remnants of which I still have to this day.

Just in case I got bored with those, I could always resort to playing with my new set of metal trucks, a box of dominoes, or the Chinese checkers I'd received, not to mention the usual array of new shirts, socks, and pants that little boys typically get for Christmas.

So for me, Christmas of '58 was going to be more about the BIG TRIP, and not the BIG PRESENTS. And I was not disappointed. Driving across Illinois was pretty boring, but once we hit Missouri, the beauty of the hilly Ozarks helped cure what ailed me. I think we even got some Black Cat firecrackers, to blow off on New Year's Eve.

Back then, I wasn't really aware just how little money my father made; all I knew is that we always looked for bargains. So naturally, come nightfall, my parents began looking for the least expensive "cabins," to spend the night. I recall we settled on a nondescript little cluster of cabins just off the highway, nestled under some giant oaks and pines, for the princely sum of $8 a night. We were charged $6 bucks for the one-bedroom cabin, and another $2 bucks for the roll-away bed my sister and I slept on. My Wisconsin grandparents shared their cabin with Aunt Joyce.

Up early, I could hardly wait to reach Texas. Traveling down Route 66, we intersected Hwy. 281 near Oklahoma City, and began our descent through Oklahoma and down the spine of Texas. I still remember the exotic-sounding names of the towns along the way: Eureka, Cuba, Rolla, Lebanon, Joplin, Big Cabin, Broken Arrow, Chickasha, Scotland, Jacksboro, Hico, Lampasas, Mineral Wells, San Antonio, Lytle…and *finally* Devine. When we finally reached Texas, I was too young to realize we still faced a very long six-to-eight hour trip—over 300 miles—down the middle of cactus-and-cattle land, on a wild and hilly two-lane highway.

I don't recall exactly when we arrived, but suspect it was well after dark. I think a hot meal was probably awaiting us and I suspect fried chicken and mashed potatoes were on the menu, being my family's favorite meal. I'm certain I was quite hungry, too, after a day of eating nothing but pre-packed fruit, and home-made peanut butter-and-jelly sandwiches in the "way back" of the station wagon, shared with my habitually quarrelsome baby sister. In those pre-McDonald's days, I don't think our family ate out at a "real restaurant" until I was at least ten or twelve.

Higher up on my agenda than food, however, was the trek out to the turkey yard with my

Grandpa Wipff the next morning. Being quite familiar with the activities and goings-on at Grandpa Hubbard's Wisconsin dairy farm, I was eager to learn what comprised the daily activities and routines when taking care of turkeys instead of cows.

It didn't take too long to discover that turkeys aren't nearly as mild and docile as grazing Holsteins. In fact, once when I'd wandered away from his side, some of the big "Toms" spread their big fans, chasing after me in genuine anger. For the life of me, I couldn't figure out what I'd done to offend them. Perhaps the mere presence of a stranger was enough to stir their ire.

Among the more fascinating activities I noticed Grandpa Wipff engaging in that day was mending some barbed-wire fencing with strips of wire, using a shiny new wire-cutter. Though I'm sure such tools existed on Grandpa Hubbard's dairy farm, I was amazed at how sharp they were, and how deftly my Texas Grandpa twisted the pieces of wire and made his repairs.

I quickly decided that I had to try them out myself. While I had no fence to repair, or wire to work with, I decided to test their virtues on the fist full of long, shiny turkey feathers I'd carefully gathered in the turkey yard while "helping" my Texas Grandpa do his morning chores.

I'm not sure why, but it never entered my mind to ask permission. I simply watched very carefully, to see where my grandpa kept that magnificent little tool. As he headed into the house, through the mud room, I saw him shove it into the drawer of an old wooden desk, which served as a receptacle for various tools and hardware. As soon as he disappeared inside the kitchen, I quickly retrieved it and began cutting away on the feathers, delighted at the fact they were just as effective on feathers as they had been on wire.

But no sooner had I started my exciting new activity, than I heard a loud, angry voice … and froze in my tracks.

"What do you think you're doing, young man?" queried Grandpa Wipff's gruff, German voice. "Give me that right now," he demanded, pulling the wire cutters from my hands. As I recall, he gave me a couple of quick swats on the bottom, too, and continued to bawl me out.

Petrified, I was now crying uncontrollably. For the life of me, my seven-year old brain couldn't figure out what I'd done wrong. Obviously I had little or no concept of what might threaten my personal safety, and Grandpa Wipff simply didn't have the patience or inclination to explain his concerns about my safety, after grabbing away the wire cutters. He had been successful at keeping me safe, however, which I only came to appreciate much, much later in life.

At that point in time, all I knew was that I'd done something *really* wrong, but couldn't figure out what it was.

The next thing I knew, Grandpa Hubbard came into the room with his handkerchief, and helped me blow my nose, which was running to beat-the-band by now. Facing me, he bent down on one knee, looked me straight in the eye, and said in the most soothing tone, "You *are* important …

and you *do count!*"

Immediately, I stopped my sniveling and began to breathe again. As I recall, I also hugged my Wisconsin Grandpa's neck, and didn't let go for quite awhile.

As I said before, I have no memory of what material gifts were under the tree for me that year. I'd already been given the most important gift a young boy could ever receive—the gift of unconditional love from his grandfather.

I'm not sure how many times in my life I've replayed that scene in my mind— probably dozens, if not hundreds. Because every time after that when classmates, teachers, or bosses were rude to me or unkind, rejected me, fired me, or left me feeling abandoned and all alone, Grandpa Hubbard's affirmation would come back to me like a warrior's shiny sword, fighting off the feelings of hopeless, depression, rejection and despair.

In fact, in some ways they echo God's message to us in John 3:16, the first scripture verse most Christians learn and commit to memory—for the very same reason. We *are* important, and we *do count.* If we didn't, Christ would not have come to teach us his ways, and demonstrate His unconditional love by dying for our sins.

So thanks for those kind words, Grandpa Hubbard. And thanks, too, Grandpa Wipff for keeping me safe. I now know you felt the same way about me as Grandpa Hubbard, but simply didn't have the words to communicate in a way that a frisky seven-year-old could understand. Today, I'm *still* grateful for the blessings you gave me—the Christmas of '58.

THE GIFT

Kim Kelley

There are writers in the SCRIBE group who, for one reason or another, have never been able to attend a single one of our meetings. Kim Kelley is one of them. Yet she felt a kinship and a common purpose with us, even though she could not be physically present. I like the idea that our group is not bound by geography and I'm glad Kim wanted to participate in this project.

I read in one of my "help" books about gifts we receive from God. I believe it came from *Captivating*. The author speaks of an account where she asked to be shown a "gift" much like her husband had been shown a "gift" of a beautiful whale seemingly splashing and spewing just for him one day when whales weren't supposed to be in season. The author, a little jealous of God's attention to her husband, decided to ask for her own whale spotting. She went to the beach, waited for the whale, and after realizing she wouldn't see one, she left. As she left, she encountered a large number of starfish scattered on the beach. She realized, quickly, that her husband's gift had been just that; *his* gift. She knew that the starfish were her own gift. After reading the passage in the book, I believed, of course, that I am so not important enough for God to stop what he is doing to show me that he cares. That's just for the special ones that matter. I moved on, a bit envious of the attention he showed them.

My father left before I was six months old. I am not asking for sympathy. Before I could crawl, before I could give him a reason to love me, a reason to stay, he was gone before my first birthday. I never heard a bedtime story from him. He never kissed me goodnight. I never spent my birthday with him. If my dad wasn't in love with me, why would God be? It is no wonder that so many statistics claim that women with Anorexia literally starve for their father's attention. I am not blaming my father, really, I am not. I am far too old to put this on someone else and have decided, instead, to take it for what it is and deal with it instead of crippling myself by blaming it on someone else. Did I need my dad's lavishing attention? Yes I did, without a doubt. Did I wait for a man, any man to "fill" me and convince me that I was good, worthy, precious, adorable, and worth his time? Yes, I did, but I realize now that no man can do that and if that is what I expect, then I suppose I will continue to keep up my hobby of divorcing because it's *not* going to happen that way. I found baby pictures of myself yesterday. I glued them on my favorite designer paper, got some hot pink and green markers and decorated the paper with crowns, polka a dots and words like: worthy, precious and adorable. I looked at that little girl, the empty one who was left, and told her she was all of those things. I cursed my father, loudly. It wasn't meant for him to hear the words. I have forgiven him and we've stumbled through my adulthood talking about mild subjects such as the weather, but I don't hold his leaving me against him anymore. He was not whole yet. It was okay for me to curse him out loud with no one to hear me, though, because I was and I still am tired, really tired, of the same pattern of needing a male figure to hold me up, love me, fill me and convince me that I am good. Love is not going to come from an earthly male but only from my Father whom I call God.

Today, I am going to risk my doubt of self-worth. I am asking for God to bring a gift just to me, to show me that just because I am me, His daughter, that I am worthy, loveable, precious and a princess and because of that, I have no doubt, a gift will be revealed to me in the same relevance of that whale or those starfish. I am trying not to be afraid to ask for a reminder that He hears me. Someone was there, a male figure, all those nights when I wanted my daddy to kiss me, dance with me, tuck me in or read me a story. *He* was there, preparing me for His work, and whispering in my heart that I could remain hopeful and that someday, I would realize He was there all along.

Ever since God put the concept of *Saving EVE* (my second book) into my head, the serpent (snake-like creature that convinced Eve to eat the apple) theme has been loud and clear. There was an excerpt earlier in the book about my jumping into the river a few months ago to get to the "pretty" rock instead of loving the one I was on. Just as I was about to jump, a large snake swam in front of me, reminding me why I didn't want to get in the damn water anyway. I had really been listening and praying that I should just trust that I'd be safe getting to the other side and thought my "courage" to take the jump was a firm foundation of my belief in God and I was so disappointed when *He* put the snake in my path instead. Later, I realized the message may just have been that I needed to stay put instead of taking the joy out of the rock I was on and only focusing where I thought I should be! I was honored, that he took the time to make that happen so I knew he was actually thinking of me.

So, back to my story of the gifts. I went to my favorite hiking spot again today. Where would *you* go to look for your "gift?" I have been pretty weepy lately but I am not sure why. My big crocodile tears always well up deep down inside of me when I visit this beautiful trail. The hike seems to some-how heal me. Six inches from my next step, a very large, long snake slithered directly across my path. I jumped, I cussed, and I walked quickly with fear greater than you know as I tried to walk away from it. I was right in the middle of my hike with nowhere to go but onward. After about ten minutes of a very intense, bone-chilling freak out session, shaking hands and walking with my knees so high up in the air, I decided maybe I should run a little to get through the dark sections of the trail where most of the path is overgrown. Somewhere in between mile three and four of my run, I dropped my water bottle on purpose because I wanted my hands to be open and prepared for whatever was coming my way, just in case. The thought of the "gift" crossed my mind a time or two. I tried to be very metaphorical and focus on a few butterflies that flew with me during my freak out. "Maybe these are my gifts," I thought to myself. The trail got thinner and thinner and the grass got a little higher. Two inches in front of my foot was an enormous black snack with a diamond head about 8 inches above the rest of his body staring right at me. I think I turned around in mid air and I know for a fact I ran as fast as I could in the other direction (which was, by the way, headed *toward the other snake!*) If anyone had seen me, they would have thought a villain had tried to attack me. I was crying while running as fast as I could. When I simply couldn't run anymore, I stopped to catch my breath but my hands, my body, my heart, were shaking so much that the real fear of dying entered my mind. I was alone, with snakes, and had to keep going in spite of myself.

I literally looked the serpent in the eye. He stared at me as if to say, "Don't I scare you?" and I stared at it as if to say, "Aren't you going to run away?" It was a head-on confrontation that lasted maybe a millisecond. What exactly was the message or the "gift" that I had experienced? I am still figuring that one out. Was it my "gift" to be tempted to get mad at God for a "lame" gift or was it awesome that I could see that the serpent was trying to lie to me and tell me that I wasn't worth that gift after all? I *knew* he was lying to me and I know my gift is still coming. The day is not over, nor is my life.

I had a friend who stayed on the phone with me while I tried to walk back with trembling hands, near-paralyzing fear, bloody, blistered feet from running without socks, and big baby tears so large that my shirt was soaked. He didn't tell me I was overreacting, stupid, too much or ridiculous. Instead, he cared for me just the way I was at that moment. Maybe, just maybe, *that* was the "gift."

Dear God, I love you but can we please be done with the snakes?

If it didn't happen to me, I wouldn't believe the story I am about to tell you. Given the history of the Serpent in my life, wouldn't you know he wasn't quite done with me? This time, the power and glory he tried so hard to accomplish backfired on him.

I have met an amazing man, who—God willing—is "the one." After a ridiculous-yet-painful argument about people from our past, we broke up. He told me his heart had closed for me. That day, my soul began to rip from the seams of my heart again. He was finished. Already. He was gone, or so I thought.

After blocking his phone number, email and text messaging from my phone, I had broken away from him and tried to move on. Out of the blue, for no reason, I unblocked the texting option and one hour later, I received his message.

"Please call me, he said. Something happened this morning that may have something to do with you." I quickly unblocked the ability to call him and dialed his number with some seriously shaky hands.

He began to explain to me the events of his morning. As he opened the door to his second floor apartment, a black diamond-head snake hung proudly on the wall in front of him, spreading his full four foot long body against the plaster. The snake crawled down, coiled up and looked at him as if to say, "She's gone. I did it. Your daily prayers together are now over. I have won. You left her." After running inside for a broom and a can of pepper spray, he attempted to fling the snake down the stairs but it began to strike. After using the pepper spray, he was able to gather the snake on the broom handle and toss him. He never saw that snake again.

We are happily together now. We know God has a plan for us. We know the Serpent can attack at anytime but we know how to protect ourselves, opening the door each morning with the power of God and His glory within us and knowing, without a doubt, that the serpent will not be there to greet us.

S. S. DOZIER, ESQUIRE

Murlene Johnston

It's jarring to learn that our view of members of our family is not necessarily the same as other people perceive. Murlene shares this remembrance of her father, whose sixth-grade education did not prevent him from appending "Esquire" to his name when he felt the need for some extra clout.

The note was written on a scrap piece of paper. The message was short and terse: "Get yourself home today," signed S. S. Dozier, Esquire. I took the note from my brother-in-law's hand and realized that today, the very Saturday that I wished to stay in Knox City for the night, I was being forbidden by my daddy. I was only ten miles away from where I was being reared in the countryside west of town. I was mortified. Here I was, a 15-year old, who would be a Senior in High School in the fall. I was being deprived of hanging in town to socialize and dance with my familiar schoolmates, and maybe even one or two graduates, if I was lucky. Besides, who did my daddy think he was? What preposterous temerity, signing his note, "Esquire." Why didn't he just sign it "Daddy?"

Esquire was a form of address used in England, a title that a man might use in very formal correspondence. In Great Britain, Esquire implied that a man was considered a gentleman of breeding, learning, deportment or property. Was my daddy any of that? True, he owned 416 acres of farming and pasture land that butted the Salt Fork of the Brazos River on the west side. He had served his country during World War I in the 55th Coast Artillery Corps. He had enlisted for service in 1918 just as soon as he became 18 years of age in Haskell County, Texas; the county where he was born, and where he spent his entire life. He told my daughter about his Army service when he was sent to Camp Lewis in Washington state. His duty was to ascend in a balloon to view the coastline in search of enemy ships approaching. He loved that exciting form of life. And I'm sure he did get some street-learning, if not education, while in the service. While undergoing boot camp deep in the heart of Texas, he and some fellow soldiers were thrown in jail in Mexico for disturbing the peace while under the influence of ol' Jim Barley, the taste for which never left him. I suppose that is why my daughter and he enjoyed such camaraderie, though she can now celebrate sixteen years of sobriety.

My two daughters could relate much better to him than I. I have an interview that my older daughter conducted with him about his life, wherein he told about his grandmother being at least one-half Indian, and perhaps even full-blooded, though whether a Cherokee or something else, no one knows. Indians lived across the Brazos River when he was born, and all they wanted from the white man was tobacco (baca, they called it) and sugar.

Daddy always bragged about being able to out-figure anyone, and certainly any one of his kids, even though he had quit school after the sixth grade. He bet a friend a pint of whiskey one time that he could out-figure him as to how much material it would take to build a barn 15'x26'. Well, he had to graciously pay that debt, for he had built only half a barn with his figures. He never challenged me because that was one of my best subjects in school.

Mother always told me that I was his favorite child, though I failed to believe such. I think she was trying to evoke a better attitude from me than fear toward my father. He was a stern figure, so much like his mother. He corrected the noise we children made while he was reading the newspaper in the evenings after work and supper, by simply clearing his throat—*harrumph*—and if that did not do it, he would say "That'll do!" and we children would acquiesce. The military hierarchy had penetrated his psyche to the extent that it ruled his idea of how a father should be the commanding officer of his family. His mother's example probably influenced him also. She had been widowed at age 32 with six children to raise, ages two to twelve. She had been ruthless with the buggy whip; one time she tied Daddy to a post and whipped him until blood ran down his legs, something that he never forgot. He was never that violent nor unreasonable, but it's little wonder that he was so withdrawn.

He didn't really desire to cut himself off from any opportunity to become close to anyone. He was just afraid and untrusting. Mother never failed to greet him at the back door when he came inside at mealtime, kiss him and say "I love you". His response was a motionless figure with arms hanging at his sides. Occasionally he might utter "A hell-of-a-way you have of showing it." Other times he would raise his foot as if to kick her in the butt as she turned to finish getting the food on the table. If that was his humor, I'd say he had none. Her naked expression of love must have convicted him of his shortcomings, his cold personality and his stiff manner. I seldom felt comfortable in his presence. The art of conversation was never practiced in our household while growing up, only orders and obedience.

My Aunt Avis, Daddy's sister, told me recently that once when I was about three years old, everyone was out in the field at my Grandmother's place. I was crying for some reason, which I did a lot of when small. Daddy came over to me and said "Cry louder! Come on, really cry!" and I said "How would you like it if you were crying and someone came up to you and said, 'Cry louder?'" I find it hard to understand that I, as a child, could be so defiant, when I always stood in awe of him. I felt that he was such an authoritarian person that there was no softness nor tenderness in him.

One morning as we three children were readying to catch the school bus, Daddy came storming into the house with his belt drawn, determined to whip every one of us, because he was certain that one of us had misplaced the rope that he needed immediately. I was just as determined as he; I was *not* going to receive punishment for something that I did not do. I ran from him as he neared me, arching my butt forward so his belt could only hit my dress tail.

He sometimes took us to the community gatherings to watch a softball game on Sundays. Returning home, he would ask if we enjoyed the afternoon. Then he would take the joy away by reminding us that tomorrow was a work day, which would not be so enjoyable.

He seemed to mellow a little and become less harsh as we children became older. I was able to ask his help with a bookkeeping problem I had in High School, and he inundated me with the solution. A group of us high school freshmen girls were in Knox City around 11:00pm one night. All was calm and not another car in sight. We got into trouble by blowing the car horn loud and long as we sped out of town. To our surprise, the night watchman stepped out from nowhere, started swinging his lantern to halt us, threatened to throw us all in jail and not allow us to even talk to anyone, much less our parents. He put fear of the law into all of us. I was so scared that I don't even remember how we escaped, but I told my parents about it the next day, and later, Daddy came to me to say "The next time something like this happens to you, Baby, just come to me and I will handle it for you."

He called me "Baby Doll" from the time I was born, because I was the first girl born to him and Mother. They already had a son. Later, he dropped the "Doll" and called me "Baby" until his death. When I gave him a birthday party at his place on the lake to celebrate his 80th year, he danced a little jig to show his appreciation. I urged him to do it again, so that I could make a picture, but he gasped "I...can't...do it...again!" After the catered lunch and near the end of the day, he came to me with his opened wallet and asked "How much do I owe you, Baby?" to which I replied "Nothing, it was my treat." He was able to accept that without protest.

I was the one whom Daddy called the year he divorced Mother, inviting me and my family to come spend Christmas Day with him and his new wife, Evie, his childhood sweetheart. It was a very pleasant day, good food, and good company. I marveled at how much he had changed. He allowed Evie to quiz him incessantly about some neighborhood happening in years gone by. His first response was that he didn't remember. She persisted in trying to unravel the story. I thought "Uh-oh, we're about to see an explosion of impatience here. Oh please, Evie, drop it before the tyrant in him comes out." Much to my amazement, no such thing occurred. I was shocked, and very delighted. I learned that Evie had as much humor as did my Daddy. Thus his funny, amusing quality was fed and appreciated at last. For his birthday the next year, I gave him a giant bath towel on which I had embroidered his initials, copied from his own handwriting. Evie commented "Wow, that's big enough that I can make two towels out of it." I must have given her an incredulous look, because she returned that towel to me after Daddy died saying, "See, I didn't make two towels out of it after all." They had enjoyed twenty-two years together.

I was the one who went to Lubbock to bring him home from the hospital after his lung cancer operation. I filled the back seat of the car with pillows to make him more comfortable as we were homeward bound the next day. I spent that night in the hospital with him in a lounge chair, and every time he moved, I was awakened to see if he wanted something. He said once, full of consideration, "You don't have to get up, Baby, every time I move."

On the road, when I asked him if he would like to stop and stretch his legs a little, he replied "No, just keep moving, keep moving". When we turned off the main highway onto the lane leading to the Lake, he raised up from his reclining position to say "This is what I wanted to see one more time." I spent a couple of nights with them before returning to Austin. It was amazing to hear Evie flounce into bed with him, jarring his painful, unhealed insides, yet all that was emitted from his mouth was a grunt.

He left this life a few years later, in 1984. His lifelong attorney friend gave a tribute to Daddy's selfless life at the Memorial Service; telling how he would give the shirt off his back if someone needed it; how he had been so faithful to support Cal Farley's Ranch for Boys; and how he wished to remain anonymous without any fanfare for his good deeds to innumerable others. In closing, the friend read "Crossing the Bar" by Alford Lord Tennyson, which he said was most apropos for the gentleman we were honoring that day.

My father's legacy lives on in my firstborn son. It is almost like Daddy reincarnated. Gerald is tall like Daddy and also favors him. Gerald is an outdoorsman who loves to hunt and fish, as did Daddy. That brings back remembrances of the times we enjoyed eating Daddy's fish, dove, and quail. When Gerald greets me, it could as easily be Daddy, for he tilts his head exactly like Daddy did, as he kisses me. Gerald inherited Daddy's gift for trading, his knack for carpentry, and his big heart for others. Gerald is full of humor and wit; Daddy blossomed with humor in his later years after all we children left home; he didn't show it earlier for it was not appreciated by any of us, especially not Mother.

Only, just a few years ago did my sister give me a copy of another note that Daddy had written on a portable typewriter. How long it must have taken him to laboriously punch each letter with his index fingers; I can't imagine his even undertaking such a chore. I thought it priceless, but her attitude was one of disdain because she said he was inebriated when he wrote it. It is written in his own sixth-grade vernacular:

```
GIFT,S ARNT BAUGHT IN STORES FOR PARENTS THAT HAVE EVERY THING
   A lot of things that they don't have
   They dont have children that comes to their Mother's home
   an stay twelve hours an never think of their FATHER or
   give him a call
   They dont have children who would think of calling with
   out reversing the call
   They dont have children who would spend an entire evening
   with them finding out what their life is all about
   They dont have a child that would arrange for all of us
   to go to church together
   They didnt have a child to get dinner wash the dishes an
   set their parents down to watch a movie when the ROOT,s
   were darker an the steps were quicker
   They dont have a written note a poem a picture or any
   thing made by young hand,s that says I made this espe-
   cially for you
   Last but not least
   I cant stay but 12 hours but I wanted to spend Christmas
   with you DAD would be worth 200 acres of the
   GRAND CANYON
```

It was an opening of his heart, of his feelings, which he would have been unable to do without the courage received from alcohol. He was enumerating the negligence that he was feeling from his children; regretting that he had no souvenirs to cherish from their youth; wishing that just even one child would desire to be with him at Christmastime. He felt that he had lost his place in his children's lives. The value of regaining that status would be exorbitant, but he would be willing to pay that price, even if it amounted to the equivalent of buying 200 acres of the Grand Canyon.

He received assurance that his children loved him from their presence keeping vigilance in his hospital room during his lung surgery stay. He showed his appreciation by keeping them laughing, entertaining them vocally with his yarns, and cutting-up. Nurses would sometimes rush to that room when they heard the commotion, for his room was on the terminal floor, where laughter was in short supply.

MY LIFE AS I KNOW IT

Marie Monroe

I was fortunate to be raised by loving, kind parents who sacrificed daily for their children. Sadly, not everyone had the same blessing. "Marie Monroe" is a pseudonym; the author of this piece had a less-than-ideal upbringing. She wishes to remain anonymous, but she also wants to share her story…which is what SCRIBE is all about.

I am a Texan, born and raised in Beaumont after World War II into a family that always seemed in turmoil. To survive, I learned to disappear into my own little world, a world where everyone was happy. This was my method of surviving the chaos that was actually going on around me. When I was asked to write about my childhood, my first thought was to protect those who are still living because my story is not about abuse but isolation. I was in my forties before I heard the term "abandonment." Strange term, but I am very familiar with it.

Any story from my childhood brings tears to my eyes. Why? Because I am a stubborn survivor of parents who are still alive and who only recognize their own needs. It has always been that way. I have a brother whom they spent most of their time tormenting, so it was easy for me to disappear when the yelling began. I tried so hard to do everything perfectly, so someone would notice me and show me love. Instead, they just expected perfection. Always negative, always complaining over every detail.

I could have become just like them. As an adult, my brother *was* like them for awhile, but his diabetes cut his drinking short. My life changed for the positive when I accepted Christ as my Savior in Vacation Bible School at the North End Baptist church during the summer of the sixth grade. Belief in Christ prevented me from really hurting myself. As I grew up I watched other families who really cared for each other. I always thought that such behavior was strange. Sometimes I was jealous of the families but mostly I tried just to avoid comparing.

My life changed abruptly after I left for college; that is when I met my future husband. He showed me what love could become. His mom was a caring, compassionate woman who wanted the best for us. She could make me angry when she wanted us to visit; I thought she was trying to control us. See, I later figured out that was *my* parent's favorite method of managing me. They used guilt and intimidation to get results; they had a firm grasp of my emotional life.

These words come spilling out of me because I will explode if they are not expressed. These past two years a gentle giant has entered my life. He has reflected Christ into my life and encouraged me to seek God. His guidance has helped me to establish my confidence and help me to forgive my parents.

I have been shaped by my past and God has restored my soul each time I reached the point of no return. I don't know if anyone here can identify with my version of life, but I am here and still standing because of Jesus Christ. My Lord has saved me over and over from my self-inflicted despair and my outrageous anger.

Growing up in East Texas before air conditioning leads one to improvise ways to stay cool in the classroom. I can still remember that oscillating fan in Ms. Smallwood's algebra class. It was so hot and steamy that my arm would stick to the desk as we took notes. Ms. Smallwood was of a religious order in which the ladies did not cut their hair and they wore dark, drab shapeless dresses. She knew her math, I did not, and I barely survived her class. I remember her because of her kindness towards me.

My father, the high school coach and a war veteran, was greatly admired by many people in our home town. They did not know the real man with whom they idolized. Our home life such as it was, caused my brother and I to search for freedom outside the family. As you can see I am venting private thoughts in a public forum. I am just a survivor with a great deal of anger towards the circumstances that shaped my life. I was the shy daughter that had been told my job was to be seen and not heard. I was basically in the way most of the time. It has taken me the whole of my life to finally become a confident adult. I am still dealing with my parents; I can do this because I am a woman who continually seeks to God.

In my journey of life, I had to learn how to have compassion for others. None was ever given to me so I did not know how it was done or what it was. My family life taught me that compassion makes one weak. I have since learned that compassion is the best gift of all. I learned not too long ago that to believe in God means not believing in fear. Too bad the negative people of this world cannot figure that out. What I want to share with those who have a similar past is that compassion really comes from God. God loves and wants the best for us. It seems to me our life's work should be to choose God's will over our own. After all, how we live our life is really the journey.

1965

Scarlett Spivey

There are several stories in this anthology about family. It's such a formative force in our lives that it's no wonder writers seek to harvest fruit from the family tree again and again. And though grandparents are notorious for spoiling their grandkids, they may also know just how to unspoil them, as Scarlett learned.

"This can't be the place."

"There's no signage, no entrance."

"I can't leave my kids here."

These were just a few things I remember hearing my mother, a single parent, say as we drove up to the camp site my brother and I were to attend for the week.

It was true. There was no entrance; it was more like a pathway where others had driven vehicles over stretches of tall Johnson grass and other Central Texas weeds leading to something unknown. Ahead, we could only see trees, scruffy bushes, and footpaths. And behind, a few cars were beginning to stop at the same location we had.

The year was 1965; post-JFK and pre-lunar landing. We no longer wore Bobbie socks and we didn't know about sit-in's. The Beatles landed, Elvis gyrated and the hi-tech "want" for teens was a transistor radio.

Teenagers also craved time away from parental supervision and looked forward to any amount of independence, if only a week away at summer camp. This trip was my brother's first and marked my third summer camp. From my limited experience, the two previous summer camps had little in common with this one; my initial impression of this camp was a total lack of any cosmetic appeal.

However, even with my mother's stirring comments and my eyes staring at the lack of anything resembling a traditional summer camp, I still found myself interested in pursuing this new adventure and gaining a new experience far from my Gulf Coast small-town roots.

Our trip to camp began after a brief two-day visit with our grandparents at their home in Austin. Offering to drive us to the camp site, my Papa loaded our gear, with my mom in the front seat and my brother and me in the back seat of a used—but still nice—white hard-top Cadillac Seville. While riding in Papa's car, my brother and I always felt special when we were noticed by others on the road. We pretended to be rich, appearing something other than what we really were— just ordinary kids in a middle-class family.

In contrast, Papa's life as a child was typical of most American children born in the early 1900's. Farm life was both difficult and unpredictable; his parents struggled to fill his hungry stomach and that of his four growing brothers. The basics of everyday life for us, just two generations later, were a given. My brother and I always had food to eat, clothes to wear and shelter overhead. How shallow for us to feel "important" if only during a 30-mile road trip from Austin to the camp site near Georgetown!

After the initial shock of seeing the primitive encampment, the four of us were led through the brush to a cleared area that would serve as the kitchen. It was simply a four-staked tarp with two long folding tables placed at a 45 degree angle under a khaki canvas. Wooden boxes, stacked about two feet high on one end of the table, served as cupboards for our cooking utensils and equipment. We learned that we would soon build a cook-pit, a girl's latrine and a boy's latrine. Prior to our arrival, we did know this much: we would sleep in tents, prepare our meals, hike to a swimming hole, study God's word and acquire appreciation for the outdoors.

Papa's yearning for growth and exposure to new possibilities gave birth to a similar desire for his grandchildren. A self-taught man, without much education, he read as much as he possibly could to teach himself. Due to necessity, learning how to earn money became his primary focus. This led him to study and collect rare coins. Through his reading, he learned the value of some coins was due to a rareness in the copper or silver mixture of a particular coin or the limited quantity produced in a given year. To share his love of coin collecting, and hoping to spark an interest in one of us grand-children, he offered each of his five grandchildren $100—a princely sum in 1965. This money was to be used only at a bank for the sole purpose of buying rolls of coins, and then spend time searching through the rolls for the rare, collectable, and valuable coins. His goal was to teach us something new and point us in a different growth direction.

Papa showed pleasure in his broad smile when he heard it was time for my brother and me to delve into our first camp experience…as the counselors began to issue each camper a shovel. Quickly, Papa and mother hugged us and then began walking back to the parked car. Familiar waves of his cigar smoke lingered in the warm and still air, encouraging me to breathe deeply and savor the sweet scent of his tobacco as they departed.

The bone dry caliche-filled soil was difficult and near impossible to break. What began as something new and fun soon became a challenging chore. The soil had deep cracks from months of dry weather and yielded no mercy to our test of jumping in the air about a foot high with the intent of landing both feet on the top lip of the shovel. The piercing of the dry earth was slow and tiring.

In time, we completed the cook-pit and two latrines; while leaving much to be desired, they at least fulfilled the intended purpose. The girl campers chose a secluded spot for our "bathroom" and in girl-like fashion we gave it as much flare as nature would provide for some beautification. The boys couldn't have cared less what the roll of toilet tissue would sit on or hang from, but the girls wanted our spot to have a decorated, feminine touch.

Our camp life consisted of rising with the sun and adjusting to the absence of electricity and running water. Without knowing, we were learning how to use our natural resources wisely and not take them for granted. When a rain shower passed overhead, we quickly produced any round container from the kitchen and collected the precious drops. This saved additional hiking trips to the main road for our daily water allotment that was dropped off in gallon containers.

Groups were assigned specific tasks to keep the camp functioning. We prepared our meals, cleaned our campsite, and bathed in streams; but we mainly had *fun* being kids. We found a stream which had a slow-moving rapid area that we body-surfed through. And we enjoyed sitting near the water's edge and hearing the trickling sounds as the water moved over and around the small rocks and pebbles as the flow continued downstream. We held evening vespers around campfires, roasted marshmallows and chased fireflies. And we all experienced the feeling of satisfaction at being able to take care of our needs in a wilderness setting.

As the week drew to a close, and goodbye's were said, I knew I would never forget this summer camp experience, the friends I made, and the lessons I learned about myself. And today, it remains in my top favorites list as something I would do again if given the opportunity.

Today I am a grandparent called "Nana." I, too, yearn for growth and exposure of new possibilities for my grandchildren and hope to pass on the desire for continued learning and discovery.

This much I know I learned for sure: had it not been for my Papa's presence and his urging to my mother, "Let them stay and build character", I'm not sure she would have let us out of the car... much less stay out in the wilderness for a week.

MEMORIAL DAY

Bob Moore

Bob wrote this piece just as SCRIBE was beginning in 2010 and he read it at one of our early meetings. He read it to us again at our meeting on Memorial Day weekend this year. It's worth repeating, even on non-memorial days.

Today is Memorial Day. The President laid a wreath in Arlington cemetery. Politicians made speeches, there was a parade downtown and the smell of bar-b-q drifted through the neighborhood. Beer and charcoal sales hit a high for the year. Stores advertised the sale of the century. It is a day for having fun. But for a few of us, it's also a day for remembering, remembering real people in real uniforms in a real war. Three of them from my childhood reappear in my memory every Memorial Day. They were my friends.

I was taken to live with Big George, my uncle, after the death of my father and the hospitalization of my mother. Big George was well liked and kind when he wasn't drinking but in the evenings, after he came home from work, he had, as they say, a drinking problem. He was not a happy drunk; in fact, he was a mean drunk. Little George, his only child, would run and hide from his father who apparently imagined that Little George had committed all kinds of transgressions. When Little George was found, there would be hell to pay; he was covered with bruises and ugly red welts on the back of his thighs. I did my best to help him as long as I lived in that house, throughout the fourth grade. Before he graduated from high school, Little George enlisted in the Marines with the help of a signature from my grandfather. He lost a leg on Iwo Jima. After his discharge, he enrolled in college and went on to become a dentist. It wasn't long, however, before he shot himself in the middle of his forehead—a casualty of war long after the armistice. He was not yet thirty years old. Little George was my friend.

Martin Reed—he never used just his first name—Martin Reed Smith was three years older than I. In the sixth grade, I went to live with the Smith family on their farm. I had never lived on a farm before but Martin Reed quickly took me under his wing and began to teach me many of the things a farm boy needs to know—how to milk a cow, split wood, trap rabbits and hitch up the mule. He made my life fun and joked with me when I was sad or lonely for my parents. Martin Reed was a rock. He was my rock. In 1942, after I had moved on and he became of age, he answered his country's call and enlisted in the Army. A few short months later, Martin Reed died at the invasion of Anzio, Italy. His body was never recovered. Martin Reed was my friend.

Earl Gilson was my hero. He was the twelfth-grade tailback and captain of the high school football team. I was the skinny and shy eighth grader. Earl's exploits on autumn Friday nights were faithfully documented in the *Herald* on autumn Saturday mornings. For two years we passed five days a week on the way to school, he walking north and I going south. "Hiya, kid," he never failed to speak to me. "Hi, Earl." I was awestruck to think that someone that famous would actually acknowledge my presence. But acknowledge he did and always with a cheery smile and a wave of his hand. The summer after he graduated, Earl joined the merchant marine. The torpedo from a German U-boat in the north Atlantic found its mark the following November, just before Thanksgiving. Earl Gilson was my friend.

The bands played today, the wreaths were laid, the politicians orated and the steaks were grilled. It is Memorial Day—a day for remembering. A distant war is something we read about in the history books. Most of us forget to remember.

But I remember.

I remember Little George, Martin Reed and Earl Gilson.

They were my friends.

SUMMER SAMARITAN

Glenda Rhyne

This was the first piece Glenda read for the group and I was instantly impressed with her attention to detail and, especially, her ear for dialogue. Aside from her obvious gifts as a writer, she proves adept at pushing some familiar buttons in this story. We're supposed to help others, right, Lord? But only if they're not going to take advantage of us, right, Lord? Right? Hmmm.

I hate having to stop for gas on a really hot Texas day. It's over a hundred degrees in Austin as I pull into a Valero station not too far from my neighborhood. I absent-mindedly wait for the tank to fill and am just replacing the pump handle when a voice reaches me from behind.

"Hello, Ma'am? Me and my sister just got into Austin today from Florida, and we don't have any place to stay…used up our money getting here…and she's sick, maybe with a heat stroke, I don't know; but I need to get her back to Florida. I don't care about myself, but she's really sick, and we been walking all over…."

The skinny young man has straggly blond hair and tattoos all over his arms and legs. He is pointing back to the curb where a young woman sits dejectedly at the pavement's edge, her head down on her arm, her face red. I replace the cap on my gas tank as I look over at her, a somewhat heavy girl about his age.

"I've been half-carrying her all morning, and I feel responsible for her since I talked her into coming with me. See, my mom said to come out here and live with her a while…and now I don't know what to do, 'cause she says we can't stay after all. And my sister, she's pretty sick; I don't need nothing for me, I don't care about me, but I got to get her back to Florida…"

I have the feeling he will keep talking until I reply in some way."How can she travel if she's really sick?" I ask.

"I don't know, but I got to do something. It took us all night to hitch from over in Manor to here, and…I, uh, I don't know what to do."

"You should call a shelter or the police or something," I offer, not wanting to get involved but not quite willing to seem heartless.

"Oh, we called the Salvation Army; they only have six beds for the women, and they are all taken. We called all around, and there's no place to go. We called a bunch of places."

I look over at the young woman sitting on the curb."Where did you call from?" I ask, letting my wariness show.

"From right there." He indicates the dilapidated phone booth off to the side of the station drive."We did, we called a lot of places. That's why I'm feeling kind of desperate, and she's getting sicker and sicker."

I am stalling for time to think as I ask, "How old are you?"

"I'm twenty-four and she's twenty-seven.We gave up our apartments and jobs and everything to come out here, and now my mom's got a new boyfriend—she's fifty-one and he's twenty-eight—and he don't want us to stay now, and, I mean, I don't know what we are gonna do."

As I weigh the options of this moment, a lifetime of Christian training and commitment is in my veins—the good Samaritan, the cup of cold water, give to those who ask of you…

My cautious, sensible husband is out of town. I am blind in one eye, a bit stiff, and generally indecisive."Well," I finally say in a slightly exasperated tone, "get in the car." I am at a loss for what comes next, but if she's suffering from a heat stroke, she can't stay outside. He goes over toward the curb, showing only slight surprise as he tells her to get in my car. She has a large floppy purse as she settles in the front with me, and he gets in behind her with his back pack.

"Don't you have luggage or something?" I ask, trying to be careful and sensible about something, at least.

"Well, that's what happens on Greyhound," the young man says. "Someone took my bag, my ID and everything. She's got a Florida driver's license, though."

I pull out of the station, and my car heads toward safety—home. I find myself saying to them, "My husband would kill me if he knew I was doing this.For all I know, you are going to kill me."

"Oh, no Ma'am. That's not us."

"Well, this is not me, either," I say. "I'm not used to people just being on the loose like this. We've got to get you some help though. What are your names?"

"Elise," the girl speaks for the first time. "Well, that's what I like to be called; really I'm Mary. Mary Elise."

"And I'm Josh," the young man in back answers. "Josh Philip Roberts. I left my job and everything to come out here because my mom asked me to…and then just turns us out on the street, wouldn't even drive us into town."

"How long since you'd last seen her?"

"Eight years. But I'd been in foster care a lot before then. My sister here is my half-sister; she was in foster care, too."

I remember that kids get turned out of foster care when they reach eighteen. Is this what happens to them?

"I can't believe your mother would just turn you out," I say for no reason as we pull into my driveway, a scant two miles from the station. We enter the kitchen, and I seat them at the table, quickly bringing glasses of cold water. I ask the girl if she thinks she could keep a salty cracker down (I'm improvising; I know little about heat stroke.).

My concern for the girl's health is paramount, though having these strangers off the street in my house is making my own situation clearer. Josh continues to talk as he sits at the table looking out into the den.

"I was making a thousand dollars a week in Florida. I'm a tattoo artist, really good, in fact. I lost all my tools though when I lost that bag on the bus. You know, I told you my name is Josh, but they say that's not a good name for a tattoo artist, so I go by Phil. That's better in the business."

In their presence I call a friend to ask where the nearest drop-in health clinic might be, carefully supplying the names of my charges and some of their story. Donna is appalled at my question, but starts supplying all the information she can, including how they might contact her church's benevolent fund. The young man, meanwhile, realizing I'm not getting a definite answer, interrupts.

"There's a hospital back up that 183 highway," he says. "I saw it when we were walking."

Of course, I realize. I tell my friend that we are going to Seton Hospital's emergency room and then usher the visitors out and back into the car, complete with a bag of grapes from the refrigerator and the torn-out listing of tattoo parlors from the yellow pages.

Silence is uncomfortable, so I ask the girl if she is going to be able to keep the cracker down. "I don't really think I ate much of it," is her answer.

"Where did you work?" I ask, and Mary Elise quietly answers, "McDonald's."

Josh—well, Phil—pipes up from the back seat, "I'm supposed to have a job interview in two days down on Cesar Chavez Street here."

I'm nervous, so I turn too early for the hospital. "I can't believe I've turned too soon," I say. "I've had two grandchildren born in this hospital." It turns out that Josh is very observant; he takes over giving directions that bring us to the emergency entrance. "Can you make it in?" I ask the girl, who seems to be feeling better.

When we get to the desk, I explain that she is sick and that I have just given them a ride. Mary Elise presents a driver's license to the clerk, who fills out a form and, since no others are waiting, takes her through the inner doors. Josh and I stand awkwardly in the lobby. "We've got to get you guys a place to stay tonight. I'm wondering if there is a small motel or something nearby, but I can't think of anything..."

The clerk calls me over to the window to learn if I am related to the girl, and I explain the situation, mentioning the danger of heat stroke. She seems to find nothing unusual in all this, unlike myself. I return to find Josh hanging up the courtesy phone on a lobby end table.

"There's a place called Crestwood Suites that I saw when we were walking this morning; it's not far back from where we came, and they have a place," he says.

"Gosh, I drive up and down here all the time," I comment, "but I've never seen it."

"Well," he offers, "you know where that Sail & Ski is? It's right behind that."

I know where Sail & Ski is. The place must be small and not too expensive. I can get them placed and get off to my evening meeting if this hospital visit doesn't take too long. We just need to make sure she is not in real danger. I ask the clerk if we can go back to where they have taken Mary, and she buzzes us back to room 5. When we open the door, a privacy curtain is drawn. We hear behind it a doctor's voice and some groans of discomfort from Mary. A female nurse pokes her head around and asks us to wait outside a minute. We do, and very soon a young doctor comes out, holding his gloved hands in front of him and hurrying down the hall. The nurse opens the curtain and is putting equipment away when we reenter. Mary looks bright and relieved, and as she sits up she tells us that they have removed the IUD that has been in place far too long.

"Yes," the nurse says. "She could have gone into septic shock. She'll be out in a minute."

As we walk back to the lobby, Josh explains, "Well, she's my sister, you know...she doesn't like to talk with me about things like that."

I am ready to get going now, my personal comfort zone feeling stretched to the limit. I volunteer, "I'm going to call that...what did you say it was called, Crestwood?"

"Oh, I've got the number. Here it is...but she did say they have a room." About this time Mary sails out into the lobby with paperwork she is directed to give to the clerk, but she passes by the desk and us and goes straight out the glass doors toward my car, striding confidently. Josh and I follow.

"What's the matter?" I ask. "Do you think she's embarrassed or what?"

We are quiet in the car and drive the short couple of blocks to the driveway near the motel. Josh has to direct me around and behind the larger buildings fronting the highway. I wonder how he can know his way so easily. When we go into the small office, a friendly young blond girl at the desk smiles at Josh and says, "Oh, yes, I do remember you."

He quickly says to me, "I stayed here a while last year." She takes the license Mary again offers and

There Is No End

has them both sign in. I indicate that I am paying for them to have a place to stay, so she has me hand over my license and my credit card for copying. Josh is exulting to Mary that they have a suite with a kitchen and everything. When the girl says that the cost will be $39.00, he tries to give her a high five—but she nods toward me and winks, "It's for her, not you." Then she holds up the sheet that has my information copied alongside theirs and asks if I would like my part cut off for me to keep. Indeed I would; this young woman seems to understand a lot that perhaps I don't.

"Gosh," Josh says to me, "I'd hug you is I weren't so sweaty. Can I get your phone number?"

"Uh, I don't think that's necessary," I reply rather sheepishly.

The girl at the desk asks, "Just one night?" I had originally intended to put them up for a week, but something has changed my mind, and I simply nod. Things have moved too fast for me. Mary says that she feels much better, and I hug her and then Josh while they thank me and I wish them luck. It is only when I am halfway home that I realize I did not give them the spending money I had planned. How could they eat…or catch a bus…or get to a job interview? I had just been too surprised by the fact that the young man, newly arrived in Austin and stranded, it seemed, knew his way around my neighborhood and could make things happen more quickly than I.

The next morning I call the motel to learn if they are still there so that I can take them some cash after all. "No," the lady answers. "We went down to check with them a while ago, and they are already gone."

Gone. Where have they gone and how? Such a dead end. I am left to wonder…was I deceived? Does it matter? I imagine how it must feel to be so disconnected. I am amazed at their courage.

Life has taught them to be resourceful.

Life has taught *me* to be careful.

I bow my head and pray for them.

VALENTINES' DAY, A MASSACRE.

Lauren Kinzie

There are lessons to be learned from every relationship, even the bad ones.

Thank you, to all the loves gone wrong
to all the ones who didn't belong.
the ones who cheated and betrayed
the ones who adored me
for an instant,
and then moved on,
the pretty boys who wouldn't grow up,
who offered partnership
but never showed up…
the "true believers"
with a cause,
so compelling
I got lost.
Thank you for the lies:
They helped me to see the truth
and recognize…
when to ask for proof.
Thank you,
for leading me where you wanted me to go.
You taught me the unbelievable power
of "No!",
or even, "I don't think so!"

Thanks for the flattery.
It tricked you into listening to me,
and made me feel captivating..
that feeling so fleeting…

Thank you to the Peter Pans.
You helped me define
A grown-up man.

To the medieval men
wanting a beauty queen
to clean
their toilets,
Thank you for showing me
The Road not meant
for me..

As I reflect on this Valentines Day ,
I realize I'm grateful for each
trip around the merry go round.
You loved me
as best you could
each in your own way,
and it was all good.

Thank you for being my temporary guides
on this caliche road,
strewn with boulders
and potholes.
You punctuated my journey
with lessons learned and chuckles..

Taken, all together,
A gift from heaven
of perfect love,
just what I needed,
right on time,
one helping hand at a time.

IT'S NOT BRAVERY

Dana Hood

Few of us are ready when it comes time for us to become a parent to our own parents. Dana Hood is there and has survived to tell the tale.

The day dawns slowly and I watch, as always, through the French doors that overlook my backyard, how the sun's rays slowly make their way across the landscape. In those moments between night and day, I find myself renewed and invigorated for what might lie ahead. The past behind me and a new day yet to unfold, I arm myself for whatever battles that may come knowing full well that I will always be victorious.

That might sound cavalier. I'm not a seasoned warrior with a killer instinct, nor am I terribly good at dealing with crisis. But I do remember my favorite scripture, Romans 8:28, "All things work to the good for those who love the Lord." So, with that in my mind I forge ahead. After all, I love the Lord and I know that He loves me and wants me to be happy.

But, I wasn't always that way. There's a time in our lives when we must deal with an event or circumstance that is somewhat extraordinary, even if only to us. It is then that some of us put our heads down and plow through the problem, not knowing or caring about the how's or the why's, working diligently towards a solution. Our only thought is to be in control once again.

When my mother fell victim to a massive ischemic stroke in November of 2010, I was put to the test. How would I handle the adversity that came barreling down on me so fast that I could barely breathe?

I put my head down, took stock of our assets and liabilities and proceeded to create a care plan for my mother that not only included her medical care, but the care of her household, her finances and her mental state.

While everyone around me wept and bemoaned her fate, I stood by my Mom telling her, "I'm sorry. I'm not a hand holder. I'm an organizer, a planner. I'm the logical one." I assured her that I would take care of the big things. Nothing would go unhandled.

I left the hand-holding, the hair-brushing, the bathing, dressing and all those other personal chores to someone else. The little things, those that I thought then were so insignificant, were best left to those more suited to the task.

I became the spokesman for my Mother's wishes. Indeed, as her only child and closest relative, I became her most vocal advocate. I immersed myself in legalities and medical decisions and paperwork. Mom would send me a smile from time to time when I had to "advocate" for her care with stronger words than the nursing staff would have liked to hear.

I did not stop to think about her long term prognosis. I did not cry when the doctor told me that the entire left side of her brain was non-responsive and that she would likely never get any better than she was at that moment. I did not cry when doctor after doctor would look at her MRI and wonder that she was still alive.

I never did allow myself to feel. I was too busy, too organized, too focused.

Now, with some months' distance, I understand that the weight of her existence in its current state is ponderous. She sits blithely smiling in her wheelchair, watching old movies with actors she can no longer name and titles she fails to remember. She delights in having her hair done on Fridays and enjoys the occasional girl scout cookie. She laughs at my children and cries when she realizes, only briefly, that she cannot speak. That the life she knew is gone. Those pale, blue eyes still hold more knowing and conviction than ever, even if it's only in tiny, disjointed bits.

Gradually, I have found that those little chores that I so readily brushed aside in the beginning are now the only things I still have to connect to the remnants of my mother's psyche. She is happy when I curl her hair or do her nails.

Often, people tell me how brave I am when they witness me performing these simple tasks.

Inwardly, I laugh. It's not bravery that keeps me going. I think, when trouble strips away all your other options, that which people call bravery is the little light of hope in the corner that you retrieve to light your way. It's tiny, reticent and faint. But somehow it's strong enough.

Don't call me brave for clinging to the only thing I have. I certainly don't call it that. From somewhere deep inside, I know that all is as it should be. I often don't understand, but I know with a certainty born of conviction that everything is well. In my quiet moments, I let God speak to me and remind me that everything is in HIS time, not mine. That there is a plan. It's my job to carry it out.

So I go on.

Patiently waiting for the next set of instructions to see if I can continue building this complicated contraption that is my life. There are so many moving parts. So much unknown.

I cry often now. Alone, when the paperwork is done and everyone is gone. But they are tears for my loss, not hers. They are tears of frustration and anger and all that should have come earlier on; but I just wouldn't allow them. I had no time. I allow them now.

Sometimes, when I arrive for a visit, Mom is sleeping. I look at her and ponder her fate. I used to ask why. But there is no use in that. I simply accept the cards that have been dealt, as I know she has, and I trust that in the end it will all work out.

TRAIL OF TIDES: A MEMOIR

Nancy Bode Bussey

Let's see, what have we not covered in this anthology? Oh, how about a little romance? In this imaginary memoir, Nancy sets the stage for some beautiful music in the beautiful Northwest.

Postcards on Helen's cork bulletin board beckoned to her. Paris, London, New Zealand and Bali. All were seductive places her friends visited. She had been to none of these places, but there was one other postcard that she had bought five years ago, brought home and pinned on the board. A small red and white lighthouse perched on a beach with an imposing snow-capped mountain in the background across a body of water. Port Robinson Lighthouse on Vashon Island, across the Puget Sound from Seattle, loomed magnificently. Mount Rainier, at over 14,000 feet, added a mystical majesty. The Indians still considered it a sacred place. That card spoke to her the most. Water, mountains and pine trees, she thought, were the perfect geological combination.

But would she—could she—up and quit her job? Her university retirement did not cover all of her expenses, but she was getting close to drawing early social security. I'll find a way, she suddenly thought and immediately wondered where that thought had come from?

Most folks, including both women and men, Helen decided, had similar ways in exhibiting their mid-life crises. New cars, exotic trips, delving into New Thought spiritualities, getting a tattoo, sky-diving, mountain climbing or having an affair.

Helen was six months away from the beginning of that dreaded period, the 60's—the age, not the fabulous decade of sex, drugs, rock and roll. She began to think about what she might do to mark the beginning of that auspicious decade. Oh no, it was the start of middle age. Oops, not even middle age she realized, unless she lived to 120.

Having retired four years before from a career at a major university, Helen had then dabbled in real estate. She had enjoyed it but was too uncomfortable at not taking in a steady, monthly paycheck since she was divorced and on her own. Currently she was in a dead-end job at a property management company that paid the bills but did not speak to her soul.

Helen was also involved in a dead-end relationship that was sputtering but refused to die. She desperately needed to end it and had read several books on love addiction, in-the-meantime relationships, and face-it-he's-just-not-the one. Her two sons were single and engineers and flourishing in their respective jobs, jobs that would possibly take them out of state or even out of the country. Helen was not holding her breath until she got grandchildren.

Sitting at her desk and watching the traffic go by in the mid-afternoon on a beautiful spring day, Helen wondered why she was still at this job. What was stopping her? She considered a trip to Paris along with a girlfriend or two. She certainly would not be going with Stuart, her soon to be ex-boyfriend. He did not know this. He was vainly secure in her neediness.

She looked at the postcard again of the island and mountain. That's where I want to go. She was feeling an inexplicable magnetic pull. Fay, her best friend and college roommate, along with her husband had bought a vacation home there seven years ago and Helen had visited there once or twice a year since, absolutely falling in love with that part of the country and especially the rural island, just minutes away from Seattle. The only way to get there was by ferry; there were no bridges, which only added to the appeal of the getaway.

Could I find love there? she mused. An incurable romantic, she thought, why not?

One month and a big leap of faith later she had packed her car to the max and headed west with her retired friend, Tara. Once she had made her decision, she had called Tara, with whom she had been on adventures before. Tara didn't hesitate. Just tell me when to show up at your house and I'll be there, Tara had said.

Her SUV was packed with clothes, laptop and snacks. They were travelling in mid-October so she packed sweaters, coats, gloves, hats, and jeans.

They journeyed to El Paso, Albuquerque, the Grand Canyon, Las Vegas and Yosemite before bending to the north and heading for Washington. It was a somewhat leisurely five-day trip, since they wanted to stop and enjoy the scenery along the way. Tara, an introvert, had never been to Las Vegas so Helen bid her an early goodnight and proceeded to play craps and blackjack at the Venetian Hotel, pocketing $450.00 to add to her trip fund.

Spending one night at the south rim lodge at the Grand Canyon, they were rewarded by a spectacular sunset and an awesome sunrise where tourists brought pillows and blanket to await the sun's climb over the canyon. Applause and cheers rung out as the sun's rays splashed pinks and oranges across the morning sky and canyon's walls. Helen and Tara were still in their pajamas, covered by coats.

Waiting for the south-end ferry to cross the Sound, Helen could see Vashon from the shore. Tall pines fringed the island as the sunset cast its final rays on Mt. Rainier to the east.

Helen breathed deeply of the pure, clean air that she had recalled back home in Texas during the arid, extremely hot weeks of an unrelenting summer.

Ah, she was finally back on Vashon, and it felt like a homecoming. Fay and her husband had graciously offered her a stay in their home while she made her next plan. The plan was for her to stay there for two months. She figured that by then she would know whether she wanted to stay or return to Texas.

Tara stayed for a few days and then flew back to Texas to begin a part-time job teaching art to Pre-K through third graders in an after-school care program. She had loved the island and completely understood Helen's fascination with the Northwest. They had a great day trip over to Seattle to the museum and to Pike Place market and ate alderwood-smoked salmon along with several glasses of Chardonnay.

Helen stocked up on organically grown veggies and fruits from the local farmer's market. From the ages of the vendors and their mode of dress in tie-dyed long flowing skirts, hand-knit sweaters and Birkenstocks, Helen believed that a lot of hippies had settled here and found their niche. She found some fragrant homemade soaps and candles – lavender, sandalwood, citrus balsam, and vanilla. She bought some for herself and for Christmas presents since she had already planned to fly to Austin for the holidays to spend time with her sons and friends.

By November, most of the leaves had fallen and there had been a few snow flurries. Being on the coast, the island normally did not experience very frigid temperatures but it was definitely colder than Texas. Helen embraced the invigorating cooler days and cold nights, building a nightly cozy fire in the upstairs family room.

Luckily, it was easy to meet people here. Everyone was very friendly yet curious about this single woman's adventurous move across the country. The mix of artists, writers and other creative types pretty much accepted her story of her mid-life quest as many of them had had similar stories. Vashon contained an eclectic mix of hippies, artists, multi-generational islanders and some reclusives who had sought out a solitary existence on an isolated island.

Out for a walk about town, which consisted of six blocks and one blinking light, Helen pulled her jacket a bit tighter and picked up her pace since the late afternoon sun was sinking, as was the temperature. She was starved and wanted a cheeseburger. Stopping in at a funky antique store, she asked the owner where to get a good burger.

The statuesque brunette with beautiful long auburn hair, about Helen's age, smiled and said,

"Without a doubt, go to Vashon Island Burger. Melt-in-your-mouth burgers, made the old-fashioned way, wrapped in tissue paper. Just down the block on your left, past the Presbyterian church."

"Great. Thanks. You have some unique jewelry," Helen said, admiring some pieces in the glass case by the register. "I'll come back when I'm not so starved."

She found the little red and white painted building with a sign out front that read, "Come on in so we both won't starve." Smiling, she opened the front door and stepped in the tiny building. She was the only one in the burger joint except for the guy behind the counter who was cooking at the grill. She studied the blackboard, already knowing what she wanted but curious to see what this little place had to offer. She would soon find out. A small TV in the corner displayed the Dallas Cowboys against the New York Giants Sunday game.

Wearing a navy blue Seattle Seahawks sweatshirt and nice fitting jeans, the cook—who turned out to be the owner—turned around and said, "What can I get you?"

She now actually noticed him and was met by the most startling blue eyes she had ever seen. Normally not at a loss for words, she stammered a bit before saying, "Cheeseburger and a chocolate malt, please." Wanting to say more, Helen nodded at the TV and asked, "What's the score?"

"Oh the Giants are way ahead. You a fan?"

Still mesmerized by those eyes, Helen also took in the silver closely-cropped hair, his wide smile and an immediate sensuality that was both disarming and making her heart race. Good grief, she thought. How long has he been on this island? She had been coming here regularly for ten years and had never seen this man. And it was a small island.

He grilled her burger and produced her malt in no time at all. After taking her money, he came from behind the counter, leaned back against it while Helen perched on a stool, pretending to be engrossed in the football game. She was a big Cowboys fan, but there was something close by that was much more interesting.

"You're not from around here," he smiled. "Are you visiting?"

Helen thought she had blended in pretty well with the island types and wondered if she had "Tourist" stamped on her forehead. "Kind of."

Those beautiful blue eyes looked puzzled.

Helen explained that she was staying at a friend's house for the time being while deciding whether or not to move from Texas.

Only a customer or two came in before closing time at five o'clock to interrupt their chitchat. She really didn't want to leave, but she didn't really have a reason to stay. She crumpled her trash into the can and stood up to leave.

"Thanks for a great burger. Just like a mom-and-pop place back in Austin called The Frisco."

"Hey, you are welcome. And welcome to our island. It's good to see new faces here. We mainly

There Is No End

get locals and, of course, the summer tourists." He grinned and then turned to scrape the grill and put condiments away.

Things were definitely continuing to look up. A beautiful island and a handsome man, to boot. What more could a girl want? Helen gathered up her purse and put her jacket back on as the temperature was dropping and the wind picking up.

"If you'd like to grab a movie sometime or get a bite to eat….well, there are some other places to eat on the island. A good Chinese restaurant and a pizza place. I realize you have just eaten, of course. By the way, I'm Phil." He extended his hand across the counter. His handshake was warm and firm.

"That would be great. I'm Helen." Helen smiled back and they traded cell phone numbers.

Back at Fay's house, Helen built a fire and she put on the teakettle. Wrapped up in a large black and red plaid blanket, she curled her feet under her and watched the dancing flames while she sipped on some mango hot tea. She thought about the past year and the disappointments with love relationships since her divorce six years ago. It almost took moving across the country to make the break from Stuart. They had lived together for two years and then she discovered he had been cheating on her for six months, while still living with her. A few months after she had changed the locks on her house and tossed him out, he begged for forgiveness, asking her to see him again. Helen forgave him and opened her heart but fortunately not her home again. She realized that she would never fully trust him again and that there were other reasons that her both her family and friends had not approved of him. She saw a counselor and read books on love addiction which seemed to address her situation to a T. Everyone said she 'deserved better'. She could not disagree.

Her phone rang. She almost decided not to answer because that would involve unwinding herself from a very cozy, warm spot. Reluctantly, she stretched and padded to the kitchen counter.

"Hope it's not too late," a deep and friendly voice said.

Her heart literally skipped a beat and she took a deep breath and paused just a second to gain some kind of composure. What am I, sixteen? "Oh, hi, not at all," sounding exactly like sixteen, she thought. Good grief.

"How about a movie tomorrow night? I can get my son Paul to cover for me, and it's been a while since I've taken some time off. We could grab a pizza afterwards, if you'd like."

It had been awhile since this gorgeous man had been out? Helen found that hard to believe but she wasn't going to push her luck. "That would be fun."

"As you know, the movie house is just across the street from my restaurant so if you want to meet there, you can park your car behind my building."

They agreed she would meet him at 5:15 to catch the late afternoon matinee.

Helen put on her moccasins and, wrapping the blanket around her shoulders, opened the French doors to the second story deck and stepped out. A myriad of stars twinkled and there was what she called a smile moon, a slender scoop of a crescent. Ah, this is what I remember, Helen thought as she took a deep breath of the cold, pine-scented air. I love this island. Could I also find love here? There was no hurry. It was definitely time to slow down and take one day at a time.

Curled up again on the sofa, Helen hugged her knees to her chest and smiled. She watched as the dying embers in the fireplace winked out. So far this adventure to the Northwest was really looking promising. All it took was a pretty big leap of faith.

LABELS

Bob Moore

Here's one final submission from Bob Moore. As always, he makes his point in a most charming and satisfying way.

Dave Haney talked to us a couple of weeks ago about grace. He said that at Riverbend we do not label others. Most sermons are directed straight at me. That one, especially, found its target and it got me to thinking about my own lack of grace.

I was born in Appalachia—West Virginia to be precise. After fifth and sixth grades in Virginia, my family moved to Kentucky where I went through junior high, senior high and my first year of college. "Everyone" knows that West Virginia and Kentucky are backward states, like Arkansas, only more so. They are mountainous along their common border. Hillbillies live there—poor white trash. They marry their sisters. All of these comments I have heard all my life.

As you were reading these sentences above did you feel just a little bit superior? "I would never call people names like that." No, of course not. But I'd bet that most of us do, repeatedly, and without even being conscious of it. Have you ever said anything like the following?

The flood victims in New Orleans are just welfare bums anyway.

Businessmen are interested only in profit. They don't care about the little guy.

The elderly live in the past.

I won't send my kid to that college; there are too many liberals there.

Southerners are bigots.

Old people make lousy drivers. Young people likewise. Only we in the middle are okay.

The kid with the best grades is a geek.

Immigrants are diluting the culture.

Gun owners are paranoid.

The homeless are all lazy, beggars, druggies and/or criminals.

Even though I no longer resent being called hillbilly or redneck, (I got used to those epithets in the Navy), I don't like to be reminded how many times I have labeled others with such statements.

It's reassuring to believe that our group is the superior group, whether ours is a social, political, religious or cultural unit. We sure as heck would rather be one of us than one of them. Since we *are* one of us, we require no label. All others are best labeled for easy identification. Labeling, or stereotyping, requires no evidence. It requires only a lazy mind.

I'll admit, I'm in danger of sounding like a "preacher without a stop sign," as Will Rogers used to say. Will was one of my favorite authors. In writing to a pastor in Minneapolis he said, "(I send) love to all your congregation, including the ones who are not paid up. They mean well, parson. It's just hard times. They got as much religion as the paid up ones."

Those who are not like us "got as much religion as the paid up ones." I think I read that somewhere else, probably in the Book of Matthew.

THE STRONGEST BROKEN HEART

Lori Garrigus

Lori has written poetry for most of her life. Lately, she is discovering the joys of writing prose and that exploration has yielded this character sketch of a very important person in her life.

Lilly stood six feet tall in her stocking feet. She was a sturdy woman of strength and substance, Bert's devoted wife of 63 years, a nurturing mother to Margie—their mentally challenged 60-year-old daughter—and my husband's strong, no-nonsense grandmother who raised him.

When I met her, she was 78 years old and facing the most heart-wrenching time of her life. Her beloved husband Bert was felled by a massive stroke that left him helpless, speechless, and dependent on her constant care to survive. Lilly was not only determined that Bert survive, she wanted him to thrive. She wanted her man back, all the way back, and she worked tirelessly to help him regain not only his speech and mobility, but his intelligence as well. She knew how devastated he felt having been such a vibrant man who still, at 82, played a round of golf every day. Now he was reduced to enduring the humiliation of losing his autonomy, his independence, and his sense of self.

Lilly and Bert's enduring relationship had never ceased to be a love affair, a supportive partnership, and a shelter for their family and loved ones. They were both accomplished educators —she the small town's only kindergarten teacher and he the long time superintendent of schools. They were revered in their little town of Pampa, Texas, by every single man, woman and child who had either been in Lilly's kindergarten class or had kids in Bert's district. There was not a child who was not nurtured by them in their little, dust-covered town just off I-40.

Lilly was a source of inspiration to her family, going back to college in 1939 to get her teaching degree at 40 years old, in a time women didn't go to college. Her dream of a degree had been deferred by raising her own disabled daughter, Margie. until she was sure she was old enough to be left with a neighbor. Lilly struggled to get to and from the little teacher's college in Hollywood, Texas, by train each day. It was a ride of an hour each way.

Even though she got home late in the day, she found time to play with Margie, cook a lovely meal, and then change her dress and adjust her makeup because Bert would be home soon.

There is a faded black and white photograph of Lilly in her cap and gown, smiling and radiant with pride. She stood in front of the education building looking statuesque and sure of her success. It had all been worth it. That photo sits proudly on my mantel to remind me of all that I can be.

Bert was touched by her commitment to her own growth and her family's as well. He not only loved her, but she was his lifelong friend, too, and an intelligent, witty companion who he would rather be with than anyone else in the entire world. She kept that spark alive by being an equal and a partner as well as a wife.

She remained ardently in love with him and showed him how much each and every day. She was proud to be the one woman in the world who Bert chose to spend his life with and she made certain that he always felt loved and valued.

Now life had taken an unexpected and tragic turn, but Lilly was at Bert's side doing the things they had always done together. She would do the crossword puzzles they loved, asking him the answers to every clue. He would look at her helplessly, she would tell him the answer and then fill in the squares. She would also read to him, books she knew he loved. And there was always a Bible at her side. She would find verses that encouraged and inspired.

Every day was the same. Lilly would wake up next to Bert, gently talking to him as he awoke. Then she would get him up, help him bathe and dress for the day. She would not have him in pajamas and a robe looking defeated. He would look at her with all the love he had inside, but he couldn't talk to her, although he tried. He couldn't tell her how much he loved her, but she knew it in her heart. Together they would go into the kitchen and she would fix his breakfast. She would feed him, help him learn to hold his spoon again, and wipe his chin.

Day by day, her prayers were answered. He would begin to pay more attention to their daily routine. He would endeavor to speak more each day. Although his words were slurred and unintelligible to others, Lilly knew what he meant even if just in her heart.

After many, many months of constant care, Bert began to improve, slowly at first, but steady progress was being made. While many people would just wait to die in his circumstances, Lilly's patience and love made him want to come back to being a whole man again. He began to speak more often. He started to move on his own with halting steps and grim determination. Soon he began to feed himself. Lilly was starting to see her man come back to her, diminished yes, but getting stronger every day. She had simply "loved" him back.

When I met Bert and Lilly, this was the state of things. My husband kept saying that he wished I could have met his grandfather before the stroke when he was strong and healthy, talking proudly about how incredible he used to be. I told him he was still an amazing man, having brought himself from the brink, and that he should still be proud of him. Bert was trying to become himself again. As I watched Lilly fuss over him, I have never witnessed such complete love and devotion. She was the earth angel who was there for him every minute of every day. I learned more about love that day than I have ever learned since, by watching her with him. I had never witnessed such pure and Christ-like love. She became my inspiration, my mentor, my friend, the grandmother I never had.

One night late, we got the call we knew would come. Bert had died peacefully in his sleep. We needed to come as quickly as we could. We made the eight-hour drive in seven hours, flying past nothing but dreary, drab countryside on a moonless night. We were determined to be there for Lilly just as she had always been there for us. When we arrived, she was inconsolable. She said because of her fragile heart, she just knew she would go first. She kept telling me that she couldn't imagine a life without Bert. She said she just didn't want to live anymore. She asked me if I thought that was wrong. I told her no and tried to assure her that they would be united once more in the higher love that brought them together so many years ago.

The funeral was a disaster. Lilly's doctor had put her in the hospital because of her heart and would not let her leave to attend the service. She begged, but he was adamant. He couldn't have been more wrong and it couldn't have hurt her anymore if he had stuck a knife into her heart. She sat there with me in the hospital and wept as we prepared to go to the service. She needed to be there. We assured her we would record the service and bring it back to her. As it turned out, I was grateful she wasn't there.

The big Baptist church Lilly and Bert had attended for many years, where Bert was a deacon, was filled with flowers and many quiet thoughts were related to the family. They had been avid church-goers all of their lives. The unfortunate circumstance we found ourselves in was that there was a new minister who knew nothing about Bert or his family. During the service he pronounced all of the names wrong and when he couldn't think of anything to say, he gave a hellfire and brimstone sermon on tithing. It was pitiful and a sad, sad day for our family. How could a man like Bert be reduced to an afterthought at his own funeral? When Lilly heard the recording, she was furious and heartbroken.

Lilly and I spent the day together after the funeral as neighbors and friends brought the obligatory casseroles, pies, cakes, and jello salad. She thanked them all, but she couldn't eat a thing. She kept telling me that she should have been at the funeral. I convinced her that it would have just upset her. She was adamant that she should have been there and that she was strong enough. She was. She was the heart and soul of this family and the spark that kept the home fires burning.

When we left that day, I knew in my heart I would never see her again. I hugged her for a long,

long time, telling her over and over that I loved her and she would be alright. I knew her precious heart was broken and she would join her husband soon. It is what she wanted more than anything. Her 63 years of life with Bert was all she knew and she couldn't go on without him. She died nine months later after choking on food at the senior center. It wasn't her heart at all when the time came. Just an unfortunate accident. She was ready. She was resolute in her belief that they would be rejoined in the Higher Love that brought them together in the first place so many years ago.

The pain I felt at that moment turned into a quiet smile when I saw them in my mind's eye, holding each other in a moment of ultimate bliss. God loved them and wrapped them in His love. Whenever I think of the ones I love, I see her face and hear her voice telling me to not waste a day in doubt and despair, for I have the love of so many and the promise of being another strong heart who loved without measure.

When we arrived at the house, her death had not yet become real for me. I kept expecting her to come out of the kitchen, after cooking all day in preparation for our visit, asking if we were hungry.

At the funeral, the same minister presided over the service, but now he was prepared. He compared Lilly to the Samaritan woman who met Jesus at the well. She was bold and treated him as an equal. She asked questions that seemed impertinent as well, wishing to know if he was the true Messiah. Lilly was that woman. She, too, would have been filled with questions and intellectual curiosity, treating Jesus as her equal, soon to be her friend. The minister finally got it right.

When we arrived back home again after the service, I was still grieving, but there were yet to be tears. I didn't break down until I went into her bathroom, closed the door, smelled her perfume, and saw her robe hanging inside the door. I knew then that she was gone, but I also knew she was there in spirit to comfort me as she had always done. She was my touchstone, the person I admired and loved as the grandmother I never had, as the friend I would always cherish.

Lilly is an inspiration that I will hold in my heart always. How blessed I am to have had her in my life, albeit for too short a time. Her wedding ring is on my finger to this day. It is a precious reminder of a love that knew no bounds and will endure forever in my heart.

I sat down at her dressing table and dabbed some of her perfume on my wrist. The aroma of White Shoulders surrounded me and brought her back. As the tears ran down my face, I knew that I would never know a stronger, truer, kinder, more blessed heart. I could feel her gentle spirit all around me and I knew in my heart, she was there saying farewell for the final time. Go soft into that good night, Lilly, but listen when I call, asking you to remind me of just how strong the heart of a good woman can be.

AS I LIE DYING

Glenda Rhyne

As you've seen elsewhere in this volume, Glenda Rhyne is a natural storyteller. I was caught by surprise when she submitted this brief-but-enthralling poem. I should know better than to pigeonhole a creative person, right? She can apparently write anything. I'll read it.

As I lie dying,

I am making poetry in my head

And raccoons are playing on my roof.

In the kitchen earlier

One thudded down from a tree branch

And has followed me to the bedroom,

Bristling and clicking on my shingles.

Now he traces whispers

On the sheetrock's other side.

I am not afraid.

I lie still, not at all surprised

By Nature coming in,

Watching with bright eyes.

A PIE TO DIE FOR

Stan Lackey

This is one of my favorite things. At one of our SCRIBE meetings, I shared with the group that two of the biggest-selling book genres were cookbooks and murder mysteries. Nobody but Stan would think to combine those two genres in one tasty dish. You might want to have somebody else taste it first.

Some people drink when they're depressed. Some pray. Some do both. But when Diane was depressed she baked, and she ate what she baked…all of it. More often than not, it was a recipe handed down from the women in her family, by great-grandmothers and great-aunts, all of whom were also great cooks. Today was a more-often-than-not day: a **Pennsylvania Dutch Apple Pie** day.

All of the ingredients were laid out neatly and orderly. On one side of the counter, those that comprised the pie filling:

- **5 large Granny Smith apples – peeled, cored and sliced**
- **½ cup white sugar**
- **½ teaspoon ground cinnamon**
- **2 tablespoons lemon juice**
- **1 recipe pastry for a 9 inch single crust**
- **2 tablespoons all-purpose flour**

Flour…hmm…how long had it been since Don had brought her flowers? For that matter, how long had it been since the two of them had been intimate? Was their marriage flaking and falling apart—as, hopefully, this pastry crust will? The pie topping ingredients were on the other side of the mixing bowls:

- ½ **cup white sugar**
- ½ **cup all-purpose flour**
- ½ **cup butter**

As Diane **preheated the oven to 425f (225c)**, she wondered for the umpteenth time that day already, was Don cheating on her, and if so, with whom? Gloria came to mind… She **combined all of the pie filling ingredients and poured them into the pie shell**. Gloria's eyes had always lingered just a split-second too long on Don whenever he had finished talking. Yes, Gloria would certainly be, as the police would say, a person of interest.

The doorbell interrupted her mental investigation. She walked to the front door, hoping it wasn't Connie from across the street. Relieved that it wasn't, but Diane was puzzled by the fact that there wasn't anyone standing there at all! She looked up and down the street but saw no one. Neither did she see the man wearing surgical gloves enter through the back door and empty a medicine bottle full of strychnine into the **half cup of sugar**. The deadly, odorless granules mixed perfectly with the ingredient; enough to kill an elephant, the man assured himself, and certainly enough to over-kill a 120-pound housewife who had ballooned up to nearly 150 with her incessant baking. The man left the label-less medicine bottle on the counter and retreated as quickly and as quietly as he had entered.

Diane returned to the kitchen, convinced that she was now hearing things in addition to groundlessly suspecting her husband of infidelity. She hoped the unnamed adulteress was as nonexistent as the front door visitor. Diane proceeded to **combine the pie topping ingredients, ½ cup all-purpose flour and ½ cup butter with ½ cup sugar and layered the mixture on top of the pie filling**. Suddenly, something caught her attention; a medicine bottle sitting on the counter. Now where did that come from? Did Don leave it there this morning, and how did she not see it earlier? She sniffed the empty container…nothing. She set it aside, promising herself to ask Don about it that evening. It would be a promise she would never keep.

As Don removed the surgical gloves on his drive back to the office, he knew that Diane would soon **take two 15 inch pieces of parchment paper and wrap them over the pie**. He had seen this procedure many times before. She would **bake the pie for one hour, being careful NOT to open the parchment while baking**. She would open the parchment while she **let the pie cool on a wire rack**. She would eat the first slice and possibly make it through most of the second…possibly not.

Lana would find her dead when she stopped by for the regular Thursday-at-five glass of Chardonnay. The police would, of course, suspect suicide. Diane's fingerprints on the bottle containing strychnine would help that theory along. So, too, would the "suicide" note Don had left in the home office. It said, "Sorry I can't be with you. Good luck on your journey, Don. Love Diane." He had saved that handwritten note when Diane had placed it in his suitcase before that important business trip to New York last year.

Her girlfriends would attest to that fact that Diane had seemed depressed lately. Certainly, Gloria would verify that. He smiled thinking of her. When they could eventually and appropriately be together, he would teach Gloria how to make Diane's world famous **Pennsylvania Dutch Apple Pie**...the un-laced version, of course. And, of course, he would also teach her to **serve it warm or**—like Diane would soon be—**at room temperature...and enjoy!**

THE HUSK

Lauren Kinzie

There Is No End, but we must at least draw this collection to a close and look forward to future publications. Lauren takes us out with this lovely poem which does what we cannot always do—see both sides at once.

sometimes, we hear a death rattle,

when it's only a baby's rattle

sometimes, we mourn a funeral

that is really a baptism in progress.

sometimes the empty husk

is really just the dusk

before a glorious dawn.

Sometimes, I snatch defeat

from the jaws of victory.

Sometimes I let my fears stop me.

Sometimes I'm too tired to care

that what I needed was always there.

Sometimes I forget that

while my body is frail and tiny

my spirit is large and shiny.

Sometimes I tie my own hands

behind my back

and then complain about the lack

of opportunity.

Sometimes I forget that

He is large

Enough to handle me

And that I'm not in charge

and shouldn't want to be

'cause if I'm in the drivers' seat

I'll miss the flow,

I'll miss the beat.

I'll miss

my baptism, the transformation—

from empty husk

to God's fertile ground

MEET THE AUTHORS

Bob Allen is a native Texan living in the Austin area. After a career in the finance industry, he is now semi-retired. He writes short stories and has an idea in mind for a novel. He is a graduate of Texas Tech University and is an avid fan. One of his main interests is his church, Riverbend Church of Austin, where he is a long-term member and sings in the choir. Besides being an avid reader and a part-time writer, his interests include golf, bowling, dancing, regular workouts, listening to music, travel and more.

Patty Buchanan is a certified teacher, currently teaching Special Education part-time. The other half of the day she applies the research/ writing skills she learned in her Masters Program to write about topics that interest her. Currently, she is applying two years of research on our environmental situation to writing a book for children, because the Earth "…was not given to you by your parents; it was loaned to you by your children." — Kenyan Proverb.

Nancy Bode Bussey is a native Austinite who wrote her first short story about a time machine when she was in the fifth grade. Encouraged by her teacher, Nancy found a passion in writing. Her first published, paid article was about an organic gardener; she used her six-year-old son's toy recorder to record the interview. She has published personal essays and non-fiction articles about the arts, sports, interviewing, and angels. Recently retired, Nancy plans to write more, including a novel. She has two sons, both engineers and both engaged, so she is looking forward to having grandchildren.

Joan Carson is a registered nurse with a diverse career history, thirteen years of which were focused on the 50-year-and-older population. Her interest addresses preventive and proactive maintenance of health and wellness. A driving force is experience gleaned as a four-year volunteer on the Long Term Care Planning Council in Alameda County, California, and seven years as production crew member for *Seniors Today*, a community access cable television show in Fremont, California. She and Jean Carson are parents of a combined family of five children, thirteen grandchildren and one great-granddaughter.

Joan Costello writes memoirs and poetry of her experiences: growing up on a dairy farm in Northwestern Illinois during WWII; reflection of living and traveling in Europe, far Eastern countries, Alaska, Arizona and Texas during her 17-year marriage to an Air Force career man; seasoning as a Texas Real Estate Broker; the reality of being single in her 40's; wisdom gained in her 26-year marriage to her soul mate and their 20 grandchildren and 22+ great grandchildren; and the raising and showing of Pug dogs and Arabian horses.

Denise Fitch was born and raised in a small town in central Texas. She is single and works in the administrative professional field and writes because she loves to. In addition to writing short stories as a hobby, she reads a lot, enjoys cooking, crocheting, taking pictures, checking out flea markets, and all kinds of music. She now lives in Austin. Her story in this anthology is her first short story to be published.

Lori Garrigus first wrote poetry in seventh grade, all about boys and true love. She would write them, become frustrated, and throw them away, never knowing her father would rescue them and save them in a notebook he would give her at 45. Lori's poetry has been published online and she has won readers choice awards for some, including "Moonlight Memories." Her poetry is featured in an anthology published by poetry.com. Short stories and memoirs are recent additions to her repertoire.

Lori also writes for a living; she has written for advertising, marketing, PR, promotion, radio and television.

Since 1955, when a high school English teacher gave him permission to submit a poem in place of an assigned theme, **DARWYN HANNA** has been a recreational poet, fascinated with the dual function of the conscious and subconscious mind in creative writing. For timeline poems on demand, details and points are gathered consciously and dumped to the subconscious (God's Creative Workshop) to simmer and be organized. Life-inspired poems are triggered by a single event or accumulation of exposures and surface directly from the subconscious for transcription. Darwyn thinks the subconscious, when exercised, is a miracle beyond description.

DANA HOOD writes contemporary, historical and paranormal romance. She got her start in journalistic writing, with a weekly real estate and lifestyle column in her local paper. However, she quickly bored of telling the "truth" and pursued the more interesting pastime of writing fiction. Consequently, this led to numerous opportunities in advertising, where Dana successfully penned copy for television commercials, print ads and advertorials. Currently, Dana lives with her husband David and their two sons in Austin, Texas, where they own Austin Homes & Real Estate and enjoy an active life together. She is working on numerous full-length novels.

Since earning his journalism degree from Northern Illinois, **PETER A. HUBBARD** has worked for several publishing and media enterprises, including Christian book publishers, bookstores, magazine, newspapers, websites and PR firms. For most of the past 25 years, he has worked as an automotive editor and journalist. Peter moved to Austin in March 2008, and has served as a Stephen Minister at Riverbend since January 2010. The Prodigal's Odyssey is his first attempt at writing fiction, and is essentially the introduction to what he hopes will become a series of novels detailing the fascinating "life story" of the Prodigal Son.

MURLENE JOHNSTON is a native Texan, growing up during the Great Depression in rural Haskell County. She is proud to be a member of the "Greatest Generation," though she was not directly involved in the military. Since retirement as a Real Estate Broker, she was part of a group of writers who met at Riverbend for nine years. At the encouragement of her daughter, she has written her memoirs and continues to write short stories. She moved to Austin in 1979, where her two daughters reside. Her two sons live in north Texas.

Native Austinite **KIM KELLEY** has been a member of Riverbend Church since 1987. After having her first book, *Cantaloupe Dance*, published in 2006, she continues to write in hopes that her words will connect with others with a sense of humor, passion, love and tragedy. Her hope for her second book in progress, *Saving Eve*, is to speak out to others recovering from Anorexia and to assure them they are not alone. Kim lives in Austin with her two daughters and, besides writing, enjoys sharing her faith, which has sustained her.

LAUREN KINZIE is a retired and reformed attorney, and author of the PimpinPoet™ blog. She was in-house counsel for a variety of corporations, and found, that upon retirement, her creative powers and her soul returned in the form of beautiful poetry. Her passion and mission is writing poems which tell a powerful, provocative and true story while not requiring a decoder ring to decipher. She lives with her husband, two children, a dog that thinks it's a cat, and two cats that think they're dogs.

STAN LACKEY was a DJ and then a talk show host. Because of things Stan said on the radio, he ended up in lawsuits against both CBS Radio and Clear Channel. But Stan was lost then; now he is found. He retired from radio and currently writes screenplays with a Christian writer in Los Angeles. Although Stan lives alone, he lives a serene and peaceful life, but even these can have their share of tragedy, and God has seen fit to afflict Stan: he is an avid Denver Broncos fan and continues to suffer from this thorn in the flesh.

MARTY MCALLISTER lives in Central Austin and teaches piano in her home. She has a degree in Music Education from UT and returned to Austin in 2003. She has performed in musical theater and with a number of choral groups, both in the United States and abroad. Marty loves travel and has spent the last 20 years vacationing in Europe as often as possible. Writing has been a way for her to relive the many treasured memories of those trips. She enjoys artistic endeavors, gourmet cooking and foreign languages, which she alway attempts to use in her travels.

MARIE MONROE is married and lives in Austin, Texas. She is currently caring for family and friends. Faith is being sure of what we hope for and certain of what we do not see. Hebrews 11:1

BOB MOORE is a graduate of the University of California at Berkeley with additional study at the Graduate School of Management in Arizona. Because of his Navy medical corpsman experience, he went to work for Searle Pharmaceuticals serving in various sales and marketing positions including chief operating officer and Director of Marketing for Amersham/Searle Corporation, a joint venture with the British Atomic Energy Authority. Since retirement, Bob calls himself "the world's most unsuccessful volunteer," for reasons that may form the basis for a future book. Bob and Phyllis have loved Riverbend since 1994.

GLORIA GENE MOORE wakes up every day grateful to have another one and especially to spend it in Austin, Texas, her favorite place in the universe, except maybe for Maui. She has been in love with Austin since 1984, when she moved here to work on some of the city's earliest music promotions as Director of Tourism at the Austin Chamber of Commerce. She continues to absorb as much music and Austin as she can, happy that she's still alive to enjoy it! Gloria coordinates Riverbend's cancer support group, is a Stephen Minister, and attends the Seminary of the Southwest.

LEE ANN PENICK has served as a Financial Advisor with Ameriprise Financial for the last 10 years. She has a Master of Arts in both Religious Education and Marriage and Family Counseling from Southwestern Baptist Theological Seminary. Lee Ann has served on church staff in Texas and in Kansas over the years as a Minister of Missions and Outreach and as a professional Christian counselor as a LPC. She currently teaches the new Women in the Word Sunday School class for single women at 11:00am in Quad 5A-B. She has a passion to teach and communicate God's Word.

Residing near Austin, Texas, **DEBORAH REGISTER** is a Christian mother of three. She earned her Bachelor's Degree from East Texas Baptist College and her Master's Degree from the University of North Texas, majoring in Secondary Mathematics, English, and Education. Family and church responsibilities, together with a twenty-nine year teaching career, define her life's ministry. Retirement has enabled her to enjoy her two favorite activities, reading and writing. She has been published in a professional journal and now writes poetry and prose under the pen name of Deborah Rose. She is currently working on a collection and an inspirational novel.

GLENDA PEVEY RHYNE was born in Brookhaven, Mississippi, and has an MA degree in English Literature from the College of William & Mary. She directed a State-winning UIL one-act play and served on the faculties of Georgia State University and Texas A&M, where her children, Amber and Tommy, were born. Her family moved to Austin in 1984 and became active in the Eanes School District. Glenda was a gubernatorial appointee to the Texas Academy of Math and Science advisory board, which later made her an honorary graduate. She and her husband Tom recently celebrated their 50th wedding anniversary. Tom says she makes wonderful chocolate-chip cookies, too.

Community involvement is a passion for KARIN RICHMOND. She has been active in securing tax incentives for hiring economically-disadvantaged workers for nearly 30 years. She has served on the Austin Chamber of Commerce Board, Leadership Texas Board and on the Board of the International Economic Development Council. Riverbend has been her spiritual home since 1993. She is an active mom to her teenage son, which frankly takes up most of her waking hours.

LISA SHELTON ROBERTSON was born in Austin at the traffic light at Oltorf and South Congress (Yes, really). She grew up in Dripping Springs, Texas, then attended college at U.T. San Antonio, graduating with a B.A. in American Studies—and if you've heard of that degree, she wants to talk to you. After years as a newspaper reporter and public relations representative, Lisa landed at Riverbend, serving as the church's television and video producer. Her main claims to fame are her amazing daughter, Lindsey, and her wonderful husband, Mike. She hopes her story makes you laugh.

SALLI SMITH is inspired by the emotion of life, relationships and nature, and enjoys expressing them in the written word. She has a civil engineering degree and has worked in the telecommunications field for over 25 years, where she currently serves as a Senior Vice-President. She is a native Texas and grew up in a small farming community in central Texas. She loves spending time outdoors—biking, sailing and traveling with her husband, Theo. Salli also has a passion for drawing, painting and photography.

The culmination of a career change, the ten-year anniversary of cancer survivorship and the SCRIBE group provided the impetus for KATHY SOUTHER to write this memoir about her cancer journey. The story's intention is to honor and provide encouragement for all those whose lives are touched by cancer. Previously in sales for the high tech industry, Kathy now enjoys the break from writing proposals and presentations to devoting time for creative writing, as well as pursuing an interest in landscape design. She also appreciates reading great fiction, blessed time with family and friends, traveling and gardening

SCARLETT SPIVEY has worked in the legislative and pension field for over 15 years before retiring recently. A sixth-generation Texan, she is currently working on her first book about the social challenges facing America's largest generation in retirement. Scarlett has extensive interests in genealogy, gardening, reading and volunteering. She lives in Austin, Texas, with her husband, and near her three children and two grandchildren.